AMBIVALENCE IN MENTORSHIP

Ambivalence in Mentorship is based on research of scores of mentors and protégés in longstanding relationships representing a range of career fields. Using vivid case narratives, the book takes a nuanced look at the emotional complexities of their mentorships—the intense passions and hopes that get stirred up in these professional, yet intimate connections as well as the turmoil created by disappointment, betrayal, competition, and the mere readiness to move on and separate from these relationships.

Framing the psychodynamics of mentorship dialectically, the book unpacks the relational struggles in mentorship to trace how these emerge from strong emotional bonds. This is accomplished by delineating and illustrating three modes of the ambivalent attachment between mentor and protégé: idealization, loyalty, and generativity. Pushing at the boundaries of research on the topic, *Ambivalence in Mentorship* locates this relationship at the crosshairs of authority and love—highlighting the interplay of intrapsychic, interpersonal, cultural, and historical forces that drive this relationship to be at once vital and risky. Professionals in the social sciences, business, and management fields will find that the book offers a fresh perspective and authentic voice to the very real joys and complicated feelings that attend mentorship.

Bonnie D. Oglensky, Ph.D., is a psychoanalytically-oriented sociologist, professor, and Academic Director of the Sociology and Human Relations Programs at The City University of New York, School of Professional Studies (USA).

"This is destined to become *the* reference book on mentoring. It offers a deep understanding of the experiences of mentors and their protégés, and an equally deep understanding of emotional ambivalence at work. Oglensky's study interweaves insights from politics, symbolism and emotions to account for the unique kaleidoscope of interpersonal relations present in today's workplaces."

Yiannis Gabriel, Professor of Organizational Theory, University of Bath, UK

"We all know that mentors change the lives of the people they mentor. What we may not always know is that these protégés return the favor. Given the complexity of these relationships, anyone who wants to better understand this intricate interface would be wise to read Bonnie Oglensky's Ambivalence in Mentorship. Unlike many other contributions within this domain, this book gives the reader a real in-depth understanding of what's taking place under the surface."

Manfred F.R. Kets de Vries, Distinguished Clinical Professor of Leadership Development and Organizational Change, INSEAD, France, Singapore and Abu Dhabi

"What's the power dynamic between the mentor and the mentored? Who depends upon whom? At one point does mentoring end and projection begin? Twenty-five years ago, I was mentored by a powerful, imposing, but ultimately loving teacher. Looking back, I see that he didn't know everything, he wasn't always right, although I believed he was. Bonnie Oglensky is wise to ask us to acknowledge the complexity of mentorship. No doubt many who have been mentors or mentored will benefit from her insights."

Tom Grimes, author of *Mentor: A Memoir*, 2011 PEN USA finalist for Best Work of Nonfiction

AMBIVALENCE IN MENTORSHIP

An Exploration of Emotional Complexities

Bonnie D. Oglensky

Routledge
Taylor & Francis Group

LONDON AND NEW YORK

First published 2018
by Routledge
2 Park Square, Milton Park, Abingdon, Oxon OX14 4RN

and by Routledge
711 Third Avenue, New York, NY 10017

Routledge is an imprint of the Taylor & Francis Group, an informa business

British Library Cataloguing-in-Publication Data
A catalogue record for this book is available from the British Library

Library of Congress Cataloging-in-Publication Data
A catalog record has been requested for this book

ISBN: 978-1-78220-418-3 (pbk)

Typeset in Palatino
by The Studio Publishing Services Ltd
email: studio@publishingservicesuk.co.uk

CONTENTS

ACKNOWLEDGMENTS

I want to acknowledge support from several people whose presence in my life helped me get through writing this book. Many thanks to Laurie Margot Ross for her friendship and encouragement, and for being so open to sharing her own mentoring sagas as they unfolded—providing much food for thought over the years. I am deeply indebted to Julia Wrigley, John Mogulescu, and George Otte from the City University of New York (CUNY) for their career rescue efforts—breathing new life into my academic endeavors, and to the CUNY School of Professional Studies for giving me a needed break from my academic duties to think and write. Reaching back in time, many thanks to Carol Munter for her valuable insights about transference and ambivalence; particularly, her attunement to my transference and my ambivalence. I am also very fortunate to have Eve Leeman in my life, and wish to thank her for her amazingly perceptive and caring counsel, and for always helping me feel that I turned out okay—fortunately, often enough, more than okay. To Eli Schwarz, Sarah Schwarz, and Elad Morad, my deepest gratitude for allowing me, as time has gone by, to feel more and more connected to the power and pleasure of caring for the next generation. There's nothing quite like it. And, my greatest love to Ira Schwarz for his inspiration—no, for his insistence on finding the right words, for being my emotional rock, and for his very reliable ability to make me laugh until it hurts.

* * *

Some chapters and sections of this book reflect previous writings of mine. Permissions have been granted by publishers to reprint excerpts and rework text from the following articles: Oglensky, B. D. (2010). The "M" word: fears and fantasies. *Clio's Psyche*, *16*(4) and Oglensky, B. D. (2008). The ambivalent dynamics of loyalty in mentorship. *Human Relations*, *61*(3).

ABOUT THE AUTHOR

Bonnie D. Oglensky, Ph.D., is a psychoanalytically-oriented sociologist, professor, and Academic Director of the Sociology and Human Relations Programs at The City University of New York, School of Professional Studies. Her interest in the socio-emotional complexities of professional and workplace relationships—particularly those such as mentorship that are authority-based—have led to research and publication of well received books and monographs including *The Part Time Paradox: Time Norms, Professional Life, Family and Gender* (co-authored with C. F. Epstein, C. Seron, and R. Saute, NY: Routledge, 1999) and numerous scholarly and popular articles and reviews. Prior to her academic life, Dr. Oglensky served on the executive team of Project Liberty—New York City's emergency mental health response to the 9/11 terrorist attacks and was a clinical social worker with battered women, homeless families, and school children at one of the oldest settlement houses in the U.S. She is deeply committed to bringing together frameworks for understanding how the psyche and social connect—especially, though not exclusively, in work life.

*To the mentors and protégés whose rich and sometimes
difficult stories give this book its soul*

PREFACE

This book about mentorship and the ambivalence it stirs up is, naturally, deeply personal. Lest the reader think that I am writing two different books here, however, it is important to note that my own mentorship story recounted below is meant for the reader to gain some insight about why I have had to do this research and write this book. The book itself is not based on my personal story. Rather it reflects my immersion in social science research over the past twenty-five years—consisting of interviews, conversations, and reviews of written accounts of mentors and protégés involved in enduring, emotionally complicated, and often life changing relationships. But first, some reflections on my own experience.

Starting from a young age, I noticed my intense relationships with and feelings about teachers. Certain ones were central to my emotional world. I remember feeling utterly bereft when my fourth grade teacher left mid-year to do a volunteer stint with poor children in Honduras. I remember sidling up to my violin teacher, hungering for his loving guidance and praise; he even sat us kids on his lap—something that today would certainly raise eyebrows if not outright legal charges but in my time, it never seemed naughty. I gladly accepted his warmth. And then in high school, there was my chemistry teacher, Mr. Lynam, uncommon in his capacity to listen and connect. He let me stay after class to talk. And we did—about everything imaginable, though I cannot remember a single conversation about chemistry. He made it safe for me to show how vulnerable I felt as a heady, ultra-sensitive, teenage girl trying to be okay at being different from the pretty, athletic, happy-go-lucky blondes in my grade. Mr. Lynam and I grew very close. I admired his soothing quality, his intelligence, his candor, and I was especially enthralled with his willingness to see me and know me. I realized some years later that I had not had enough of that latter quality at home. Mr. Lynam showed me that I could be known.

Relationships like these were all a rehearsal for mentorships I had during university. I began to dig deep with the help of an analyst during those years to make sense of some of the gripping feelings I was having for my professors. I idolized a couple of them, pining to be recognized, perennially over-interpreting small gestures (good and bad), demolished by critique. I felt ashamed that I felt so needy, and began to understand some of the miscues in my connections with my parents that left me longing for good authority. I tried to find a way through my study of sociology to make sense of my radical politics on the one hand, and my yearning for responsible, loving guidance on the other. It was not until graduate school that I found this.

I grew especially close to three professors while I was pursuing my Ph.D. One, a psychoanalyst and sociologist, took me under her wing to join her in the study of a somewhat marginalized subfield of our discipline—psychoanalytic sociology. Few dared to buck sociology's derogation of psychoanalysis as junk science. Brave Catherine Silver was one of them. And, then, I was one of them, too. Catherine was my first true mentor. I had never met anyone quite like her: elegant, French, artsy, intellectually serious, and thoughtful about my development. Catherine introduced me to the life of an intellectual, something I had no previous contact with. Growing up, I had never personally known anyone who was a professor, nor had my parents. She invited me to help her with her research, we wrote articles and book reviews together, and we traveled together to international conferences. She and her academic husband opened their home to me for Jewish holiday celebrations and welcomed me at their country getaway for weekends of work, wine, and beach-walking. I learned so much from Catherine about psychoanalysis and its role in sociology; yet there was so much more to the mentorship. She exposed me to a different kind of life, one where ideas and creativity mattered—where socializing was equal to deep, meandering, mind-opening conversations, often for the mere pleasure of talk and thought. She was also a social activist and feminist and so understood the contradiction I had long tried to make sense of—that of longing for good authority even while having that rebellious streak.

I was also a protégé of Cynthia Fuchs Epstein—a towering figure in sociology, pioneer in feminist scholarship, and prolific writer of classic books on women in law. Over a number of years, Cynthia generously taught me about the practice of sociology and together with other research assistants, we went about the work of interviewing scores of attorneys about the challenges women faced at their firms. The training was absolutely priceless and serves me well to this day. But the icing on the cake was when Cynthia invited a few of us to co-author a monograph, and later on, a book about our research—an amazing opportunity for any graduate student hoping to launch an academic career. Like Catherine, Cynthia's influence stretched way beyond professional grooming. I can remember feeling very welcomed at countless soirees hosted by Cynthia and her husband at their handsome river view flat. She had an astounding network of professional friends and political comrades and never hesitated to make meaningful introductions. It was thrilling to be part of her exclusive inner circle. Yet, even as my identity seemed to be getting an upgrade, there were times I felt like I was on another planet by knowing Cynthia. One occasion stands out: although many of us were a bit star-struck by it, it was no surprise to Cynthia that her dear friend, Betty Friedan, showed up (and tried to hold court) at our book party. Betty Friedan congratulating us on our book. Pinch me, I thought. I must be dreaming.

Then came Bob Alford. It was in his doctoral seminar that I fell for Bob. Brilliant, modest, delighted by the buzz of teaching and learning. Patient, rigorous, loving, too respected in our field to worry about convention. I ended up giving a memorial talk at his funeral only a few years after I had completed my degree, representing the dozens of students he had mentored over his long accomplished career. He was a master teacher. He taught me how to respect the messiness of idea making and critical thinking, the value of unending questioning, love for nuance and surprise, and faith in the social world. We spent hours in his office, his apartment, climbing stairs to his rooftop haven in the East Village, consuming ideas. Talking about life. Eating exotic, cheap food. Connecting. He was a political theorist, a do-it-yourself house remodeler, and an old Communist. Until he lost his hearing he was a classical pianist giving recitals. A man of many talents. And I adored him. And, when I am being totally honest with myself, I felt he loved me too. He shaped me. He gave me the gift of patience in my development—something I felt unable to have as the last child in my parents' household. I think I took years to finish my dissertation partly to stay connected to Bob. My friend, Alan Sokal, used to tease me that I was in "gradual school." Little did he know.

And yet. And yet, we had had our spills. There were falling outs and some very painful times. Some of the same types of conflicts happened with all three of the mentors; but each relationship—being quite different from the other—had its own kind of turmoil. My initial and maybe surprisingly sustained adoration eventually met up with disappointment and disillusionment about my mentors' strengths and limits—what they could and could not do for me, what they would and would not do for me. My devotion to them led to cocooning that I ate up because it made me feel quite special, but I knew also it cut me off from other possible learning opportunities and ran the risk of submerging my voice. It also made it tough for me to be critical about the relationships—to talk to friends about issues, to share my concerns directly with my mentors, but most of all to be honest with myself. My eventual urges to do my own thing, to carve out my own professional identity, to even separate for a time caused me enormous guilt that led to clumsy and ultimately hurtful attempts to explain my need for space. But we got through these difficulties—with relationships more or less intact—and that is when some of the greatest learning took place.

What I have known well are my own ambivalences about these mentors and my relationships with them. I could make some educated guesses about the strains in their feelings about me. I knew of their struggles with me when they pulled back, for instance, or when they became visibly exasperated, and on occasion when they were forthright about their feelings. Still, I did not interview my mentors about how they felt or thought about their relationships with me. I was living these relationships, not studying them.

The fact that I have not mentioned any relationships in which I was the mentor is not because I have not served in this role. I have. For a number of reasons, however, my opportunities to be the mentor have been limited. One relationship stands out in this regard. After settling into an academic job, I began to develop an important mentor–protégé relationship with a junior faculty member. The relationship, lasting a few years, was thorny from the start. I was pleased that over time, my colleague's cautious way with me did seem to dissolve. Eventually she was comfortable enough to key me in to ongoing harassment issues dogging her in our department. And we stayed pretty well connected in battling these issues. But when my protégé left our college under duress, and shortly thereafter, quit academia altogether, the mentorship fizzled out. In spite of my efforts to maintain contact, my sense was that the relationship had not evolved enough to sustain the employment moves. And given that I was probably a sore reminder of the university she felt pushed out of, retaining a connection to me would have been, I am fairly certain, too stressful for my colleague to manage. To my regret, this did not develop into the full blown mentorship that I myself had experienced as a protégé. I felt it had potential. I was ready for it. I was sad to let it go. Even so, I was also somewhat relieved.

Of course, I have always mentored undergraduate students in my work as a professor in the college setting. But this kind of mentoring is different than the kind I have been referring to above. Mentoring is not the same as mentorship. Mentoring is an activity; mentorship is a social relation. This crucial distinction is a topic I delve into in Chapter Two. Suffice it to point out here that while relationships with students can be quite influential—and my own, described above, are certainly a case in point—my mentoring contacts with students have tended to be relatively short-lived, education-focused, and bound by the group (e.g., class) context.

And so, I set out on my research journey to figure this all out. But mainly to herald the importance of a mentorship's potential in a person's life. The reader will see that I can be a bit cheeky about the fad of mentorship that has overrun our culture in recent years. But this is meant less as attempt to undercut the value of these relationships than it is to put them back in their proper, serious, emotionally rich place. And my main thesis of the book is that the intimacy that gives mentorship its heft, its profound impact, is also the thing that can be its undoing. Nevertheless, instead of warning readers not to get too close, I hope to show that even in the undoing, there is opportunity for love, for growth. In fact, because of the undoing, because of the strains in the relationship, because of the understanding and ultimate acceptance of the mentor's and protégé's foibles and limitations—each party has the chance to work something through, to appreciate the vulnerability of being human.

CHAPTER ONE

Bonds that bind: introduction to mentorship ambivalence

"That which makes us most alive and connected also renders us most fragile and vulnerable."

Jessica Benjamin, 1995, p. 62

T he vast majority of writings on mentorship—in both popular and scholarly venues—extol the personal, career, and organizational advantages that come with having such a relationship. For anyone who wishes to succeed at work, that is, getting into a mentorship seems de rigueur. To be sure, focusing on favorable outcomes makes sense insofar as the explicit aim of the alliance is to offer assistance. Indeed, there is extensive evidence that mentoring can be enormously helpful to a protégé's career mobility, self-confidence, compensation potential, job performance and motivation, and occupational learning. It is no secret that mentors benefit as well, seeing gains in areas such as professional visibility, expanded influence, and organizational ascendance, not to mention the lure of ego gratification.

That said, academics and consultants have challenged what they rightly perceive to be a positive bias about the topic, critiquing it for its lack of healthy skepticism. One result has been the emergence of a counter-narrative on mentoring *dysfunctions*. Citing relational difficulties, dysfunctions in mentoring are said to arise when "one or both parties' " needs are not being met in the relationship or one or both parties is suffering distress as a result of being in the relationship" (Scandura, 1998, p. 453). Some authors issue warnings, going so far as to identify *toxic* mentor types such as *the slave master, the controller, the humiliator,* and *the dumper*. Others frame dysfunction in terms of the potential for negative effects on organizational life resulting from mentorship practices that are exclusionary, politically conservative, or inequitable in terms of access to women and people of color.

While attempts to balance out the overly upbeat depiction of mentorship are necessary, the dysfunction studies appear to swing the pendulum too far in the other direction, running the risk of exaggerating the problems. That is, by splitting the positive and negative "sides" of mentorship into separate spheres of attention, the tendency has been to flip-flop from an all-good version of mentoring to an all-bad one. Calling out the *dark* sides of mentoring—as some writers have—clearly portends this risk. Just to clarify, I am not asserting that there are no bad mentoring relationships—of course there are. What I am suggesting, however, and what I will be investigating in this book is that what remains hidden in the dichotomized treatment of mentoring is a messier but undoubtedly more realistic image of the relationship as having *both* positive and negative dynamics and consequences.

This book aims to reset the conversation about mentorship, placing ambivalence—the love *and* the hate, the good *and* the bad—in the center of how we think about, make sense of, and deal with tensions in these profoundly influential relationships.

Following the work of Daniel Levinson (1978), I define *mentor* as an older, more experienced person who is teaching a younger person—the *protégé*—how to navigate in the adult world and world of work. I view the alliance as a complicated love relationship—evoking and satisfying desires for connection through the erotic processes of teaching and learning while at the same time, promoting career goals. Even though many see mentorship as predominantly instrumental—a strategic and rational (read non-emotional) means to an end, there is growing support for the notion that for a mentoring relationship to work well, there has to be a willingness to become intimate. Mentor and protégé often develop an abiding affection for one another through their work together and through their involvements with each other's lives beyond work.

The reset I am pursuing here involves looking at the intimacy that evolves in mentorship through a dialectical lens. Like other close relationships, I assume that mentorship has benefits and the promise of professional and personal satisfaction *as well as* disappointments, conflicts, and vulnerability to harm. The clincher here—and what makes the approach dialectical—is that it assumes that the former lays the groundwork for the latter. As a preview of what is to come in the book, for example, consider the ways that idealizing one's mentor can spark inspiration and the desire to learn while weaving into a relationship emotionally intense fantasies and unrealistic expectations that can provoke disappointment, grueling developmental pressures, and disillusionment. Likewise, think about how the dynamics of loyalty that produce a pleasurable sense of connection and commitment between a mentor and protégé also entangles the relationship with the kinds of obligations and constraints that bring on displeasure, guilt-inducing choices, resentment, and other stressful feelings and dilemmas. And finally, picture how the process of generativity that lays the groundwork for a mentor to make a meaningful imprint on a protégé also saddles the relationship with feelings of loss, envy, and competition. Put simply, the bonds also bind.

Framing ambivalence

Standing in the crosshairs of authority and love makes ambivalence a nearly inescapable fact of life for mentors and protégés. The nature of ambivalence, writes Neil Smelser, "is to hold two opposing [*ambi*] affective orientations [*valences*] toward the same person, object or symbol" (1998, p. 5, my additions in square brackets). In this case, mentor and protégé—two adults who come together originally, typically, in connection with their work—form a relationship. The mentor is an authority figure in the relationship, the protégé is the subordinate. As the authority figure, mentors are the ones who have power, often in the material sense when they are also the boss or senior colleague, but always symbolically and emotionally. Mentors know more and have more of something that the protégé wants (e.g., resources, networks, wisdom, skill, style, values). At the same time, authority entails reciprocity—leaders need followers just as mentors need protégés. Hence, among other emotionally fraught contradictions, mentorship is founded on tensions between mutuality and inequality.

Freud (1912b, 1914c) called attention to the phenomena of ambivalence in what could be called the original authority relationship—that between children and parents. Borrowed from a paper written by Bleuler in 1910, Freud first used the term to account for the psychodynamics between son and father within the reconstructed family dramas that became the paradigmatic scenes of psychoanalysis. He interpreted the son as both loving and hating his father; as wanting to be close to him and simultaneously rid of him; both seeking his advice and resenting parental control (1923d).

Moving the discourse on mentoring forward by homing in on the unconscious emotional underpinnings of this relation, psychoanalytically-oriented organizational and management scholars recognize that the authority configuration of mentorship resembles the structure of the parent–child relationship and as such, calls forth and reactivates its core paradoxical dynamics. The same pattern has been observed among students and teachers. Mediated by unequal power and strength, the emotional tie to parents, teachers, and mentors is ambivalent from the start because it is linked simultaneously to a desire to identify with and a desire to replace the authority figure. Although intuitively it may be easy to understand feelings of love and admiration towards parents, to help us make sense of the contempt and aggression we would do well to keep in mind how dependent children are on parents for survival. These relations, Smelser points out, "are those *from which the child cannot escape . . .*" (1998, p. 8). That is to say, they contain elements of emotional unfreedom; they connect and constrain, socialize and control, nurture and clutch, protect and surround, and they involve giving and loss. And therein lies hostility.

Although fixed mainly in childhood, ambivalences generalize readily to other real and symbolic situations. Conflictual feelings and archaic fantasies from childhood—sometimes conscious, most often not—are grafted on to current day mentoring relationships through transference. In this process, protégés relate as if reliving an old drama—wherein the script for feelings, ideas, and behavior seems well-rehearsed and the experience of being with the other(s) feels oddly familiar. Freud's most dramatic evidence of this is the patient's positive and negative transference reactions toward the psychoanalyst, evoked in the absence of any stimulus that might excite strong reactions (1912b).

Through the prism of transference, mentors are loved because they teach, support, and protect but also because at times, they serve as professional lifelines. We *must* love them—within the organizational and professional milieu they supply us with the resources to live and grow. At the same time, we envy them for what they have and we do not. And we fear them because they are stronger than us and can discipline, withhold, and punish. We also resent them because their strength and control remind us of our dependency, smallness, helplessness, lacks, and our limits. To some extent, they hold our future in their hands. And we are prone to feeling profoundly disappointed by them because it is through experiences of inevitable deprivation by them that we realize that a perfect, easy, tension-free, pleasure-filled existence is not possible. They remind us, that is, that we have no choice but to struggle to grow.

Based on the configuration I have been describing, one might get the impression that the only party to have vestiges of early childhood ambivalence is the protégé but this is not the case. Mentors' experience of ambivalence also stems in part from early experiences with authority. Forging strong emotional connections with protégés who may lean on, look up to, project fantasies, and impose challenging expectations on to them may stir up mixed feelings in mentors—feelings that may be stoked by old family dramas. Further, how mentors wrestle with ambivalence over having their own authority, power, ambition, influence, and responsibility reflects residues of past relationships.

To be clear, I do not regard the experience of ambivalence per se as evidence of a troubled relationship between mentors and protégés. Over many years of interviewing people in long term mentoring relationships, I cannot recall a single one that was free of such contradictory feelings. Indeed, some amount of ambivalence is normal and healthy in human relationships. Ashforth and colleagues (2014) astutely note that "the more familiar an actor is with an object, the richer the store of information, and the greater the probability of having encountered the object's multiple facets and imperfections" (p. 1455). Healthy relationships are more likely to evolve and last if one recognizes the negative as well as positive qualities and develops a realistic assessment of a partner. Some of the most satisfying and productive mentorships I have encountered were those in which parties had figured out ways to navigate or reconcile difficult feelings. Nevertheless, mentorships can sour when ambivalence is too intense or when the bad overruns the good; sometimes the intimacy that makes personal and professional growth possible in mentorship can lead to its demise. Ambivalence, thus, can be good for a relationship but it also can be bad—or perhaps, not ironically—both.

After examining how ambivalence unfolds in lived mentorships—the meat of the book—I will circle back in the final chapter to a more thorough discussion and assessment of the value of ambivalence in mentorship.

Mentorship stories

This book has been in the making for several years over which time I have read and sifted through many personal accounts and talked to scores of professional people about their mentoring relationships across a broad spectrum of professions in business, academia, the arts, health care, finance, journalism, computer technology, and civil service. I have carried out in-depth interviews with nearly one hundred individuals and continue to have conversations with people involved in mentoring on a less formal basis. Since everyone I have interviewed was involved in an enduring mentorship lasting at least three years and frequently quite a bit more, my aim in these contacts has been to explore the life story of the relationship—with special attention paid to the emergence and navigation of emotional tensions and ambivalent psychodynamics. While I hope it is obvious, I should clarify that I have not done a psychoanalysis of individuals who are party to a mentoring relationship. So I will not be examining individual biographies, early childhood experiences, or transferences even though they surely play a role in shaping the unique contours of the mentorships discussed. Instead, I apply psychoanalytic concepts and perspectives broadly to guide investigation and yield insight as to the emotional complexities of contemporary mentoring relationships.

In many cases, I have been able to talk to both parties—mentor and protégé. Whenever possible, my practice has been to meet with each party separately so each person can feel comfortable reflecting upon and speaking to me confidentially about the relationship. Although a number of conversations have occurred with only one party—either mentor or protégé, it is clear to me that exploring mentorship from one person's perspective limits one's ability to get a full picture of the dynamics of the relationship. Hearing from both parties helps me to pick up on areas of relational resonance and discrepancy in the relationship and provides insight about how mentors and protégés process and deal with apparent and less obvious sources of ambivalence and strain.

Notwithstanding the fact that the definition of mentorship is unsettled—a topic that on its own generates ambivalence (to be discussed at length in Chapter Two)—my focus is on the archetypal structure of classic mentorship. In contrast to some of the newer varieties, classic mentorship is often described as the most intimate and emotionally intense. Relationships of this ilk also tend to be longer lasting, hierarchical (by virtue of differences in rank, seniority, experience, and/or age), voluntary (arranged by choice—not through a company program), and offer assistance in the realms of both professional and personal development. In most instances, I have been able to identify and talk with mentor–protégé pairs whose relationships match these characteristics and thus—on the face of it, at least—fit the classic configuration.

One caveat is that since my work looks primarily at individuals in robust, well-rounded, and matured mentorships, the themes and insights in this book may not be representative of what goes on in the wider spectrum of mentoring relationships—some of which focus almost exclusively on career, technical, or political assistance, yielding less in the way of a textured emotional connection. Moreover, the book does not cover mentorships that are ruptured or terminated. People involved in satisfying relationships are usually eager to talk, but I did not expect anyone experiencing serious tension in their mentoring relationships to be open in the same way. In fact, on a number of occasions I spoke to people who did not want me to contact their "other half" precisely because they felt their relationships were in states of turmoil or too fragile for me to reach out to their mentoring partner.

Case examples and quotes from mentors and protégés will be offered to illustrate patterns. Some illustrations are representative—intending to capture what was conveyed by mentors and protégés on the whole; other examples offer more unique perspectives through particularly vivid or candid accounts. To preserve anonymity, occupations and personal details of individuals cited in the book are altered. Mentors are referred to by names that begin with the letter "M" and protégés are given names that begin with the letter "P." Individuals referred to by their real names are those from published works—typically memoirs, biographies, and essays that probe one's personal experiences in mentoring relationships.

Outline of the book

To set the stage for an exploration of the dynamics of ambivalence in mentorship, I begin the book by zooming out. Chapter Two looks at the phenomena of mentorship and the ambiguities that frame the concept of the relationship. That is, before anyone even steps into the shoes of mentor or protégé, the relationship is frontloaded with ambivalent-making qualities brought on by linguistic, semantic, normative, historic, cultural, and academic confusions about mentorship. I unpack these, calling attention to the psychological, sociological, and cultural ambiguities that structure mentorship and thus shape people's expectations and experiences in these relationships.

Three themes of central importance to elucidating mentorship ambivalence will be explored in Chapters Three, Four, and Five: idealization, loyalty, and generativity. I view each theme as a primary mode of attachment or bonding in mentorship. That is, as dynamic processes, idealization, loyalty, and generativity are ways of relating that form patterns of attachment. While interrelated, each process helps mentors and protégés forge a distinctive bond through fantasy, deed, interpersonal communication, feeling, ritual, expectation, and shared experience. Each process is critical both for relationship development and for the progression and effectiveness of the mentoring process itself.

Idealization connects mentor and protégé through love, awe, admiration, and emulation. Loyalty connects mentor and protégé through tacit and explicit promises to stand by and protect the other and through the establishment and articulation of obligations. Generativity connects mentor and protégé through fantasies about and attempts to influence, make an imprint, and leave a legacy. As modes of attachment in an authority-based relationship, each process is also rife with ambivalence. Hence, while idealization, loyalty, and generativity bring mentors and protégés into close, intimate alliances, they also give rise to emotional conflict and constraint. Moreover, each process seems to tap its own brand of ambivalence. That is, a different cluster of psychodynamic tensions seems to be imported into mentorship by each process. Hence, each process leads to and can also stymie individual development and relationship continuity and satisfaction.

Aside from the fact that idealization, loyalty, and generativity are all key relational processes in mentorship, part of the reason for framing the book around these three themes is that they each afford a picture of mentorship from a slightly different angle. First, each theme assumes a different and fairly consistent prototypical subject–object orientation: the protégé idealizes the mentor, both mentors and protégés are loyal to each other, and mentors are generative toward protégés. Each theme also has a somewhat different temporal organization with respect to the fantasies and experiences that drive it. Hence, while the dynamics of idealization, loyalty, and generativity play out in the here and now of the mentorship and are importantly affected by the everyday situations and interactions that the pairs face—each process also taps into, reflects, and is predominantly shaped by experiences in either the past or the present, or by projections into the future. Idealization seems to have a stronger foothold in the past. That is because the process of projecting greatness, omniscience, and perfection on to another reflects wishes and fantasies stemming from a very early period in life. In contrast, loyalty seems to be quite rooted in the present as a part of the everyday routines and crises faced by the parties in the mentorship. It is manifested in and reflects concerns about the nuts and bolts of exchange in the mentorship—who does what for whom in the name of standing by the other. It often is enacted in ritualistic activity through which allegiance is expressed, boundaries are established and monitored, and the relationship is protected from external threat. Lastly, generativity ties to projections about the future. The relational pulse of generativity is energized by the mentor's hopes, dreams, as well as his or her conflicts about posterity, the protégé's role in this design, and his or her own future.

A final point is that each of these processes seems to revolve around a distinctive socio-emotional motif that reveal basic existential concerns: For idealization, is it about love and adequacy: "Am I," asks the protégé, "good enough or lovable enough to be like you, oh wise mentor?" Loyalty is about obligation and reciprocity: "If I," asks both the protégé and the mentor, "stand by you, what will you do and how far will you go for me?" Generativity is about posterity, life purpose and immortality: "Will I or my life," asks the mentor, "matter down the road?" While there may be other fundamental questions that form the backbeat of a mentorship, these three seem to capture its basic emotional rhythms.

I end the book in Chapter Six with concluding thoughts and suggestions for the future of mentorship.

CHAPTER TWO

Defining the elusive: ambiguous expectations in mentorship

I have talked to a lot of people about their mentoring relationships. These alliances are supposed to be pleasant and helpful; popular books often depict them as havens from the rough and tumble politics of everyday life in the workplace. So, I have often wondered why it is that both the words "mentor" and "protégé"—and indeed the whole concept of mentorship—seem so emotionally charged? Some people literally flinch at the word mentor and want to stay miles away from identifying themselves as one, while others equivocate about whether they *qualify* as a mentor. And then there are people who latch on to this title as if proud to acknowledge some kind of glory it seems to bestow. Just as loaded, very few are willing to call themselves "protégés." Many balk at the word and simply refuse to use it, preferring the blander term "intern" or some of the newly fabricated and gimmicky words like "mentee" or "mentoree." Why is this? What is it about these words that evoke such strong feeling? And is it just the words that are charged or does the reaction to the terms mentor and protégé signal something deeper?

An inquiry into the emotional freight of mentorship—right down to the words we use to denote its two central roles—provides a compelling entry point to an exploration of this relationship. So much about this dyadic relation conjures up complicated and ambivalent feelings. I take these mixed feelings seriously in this book as I try to make sense of them. As a psychoanalytically oriented sociologist, I am interested in the ways that emotional life—conscious and unconscious—structures and is structured by social relations. In this book, mentorship is the social relation under scrutiny.

Before moving on to the book's central focus on the dynamics of lived mentoring relationships, I want to spend a bit of time in this chapter unpacking the conceptual ambivalence in mentorship *as a social relation*. This starts with the fact that unlike almost any other social relation, there is actually very little agreement on what constitutes mentorship. And this confusion is not just about language. By the end of this chapter, the reader will see that ambivalence in mentoring is propelled by inherent contradictions in the relationship foundation. These contradictions can be thought of as sociological cross-signals. Set against a backdrop of competing contemporary and historical influences, semantic and normative ambiguities, cultural spin and contortions in academic conceptualization, one can appreciate that the social structure of mentorship is quite wobbly. It is no wonder people are anxious when using these terms.

Mentoring craze

Marking the beginning of an explosion of interest in mentorship, an article appeared in a popular magazine in 1978 entitled "Everyone who makes it has a mentor" (Collins & Scott, 1978). It discussed the importance of having a person in one's corner to be a coach, confidante, and sponsor; someone who would be a link to important networks, helping one gain visibility in their chosen career field. Since that time, over 7,500 dissertations and massive number of scholarly articles, trade books, and journal publications have sung the praises of mentorship. Panels at conferences of major professional associations on the topic are a must; indeed entire conferences are devoted to the topic. In 2017, close to 100 conferences worldwide had mentoring as their central theme.

Mentoring programs abound as well. Introduced in Europe and the U.S. during the 1980s, these programs run the gamut from the highly institutionalized to the informal, spanning the corporate realm to the world of the arts and human services, offering classic one-to-one models of mentoring to newer varieties. I have heard of group mentoring taking place at afternoon teas at elite law firms, "ment-working"—a cross between mentoring and networking, two-tiered models—including mentor–protégé and sibling pairs, mentoring circles and quads, and scores of cyber-mentoring options and mentor Apps. I was once invited to a "yenta-ring" gathering—a variant of mentorship of a group of high powered professional women who lunch at fancy Manhattan restaurants to network but end up mostly chitchatting about work, colleagues, and family (hence the reference to *yenta*—the Yiddish word for gossip).

Mentoring has been transformed into a virtual industry. There are mentoring matching services and software products (e.g., "Find-A-Mentor"), pen-pal offers (e.g., LAMPPOST—"Learners and Mentoring by Mail"), and a litany of internet sites like "The Odyssey" a blog promoting the idea of mentoring as a civic duty. I have seen jobs advertisements include "Mentor" as an official job title. Capitalizing on all of this, a growing sector of management consultants have set up shop to sell mentoring kits with checklist-driven formulas for accessing and sustaining effective relationships. Businesses are using "mentor" in their trade names (e.g., "Research Mentors"); some reclaiming an early meaning of the word—using it to title publications that provide advice (e.g., *The Money Mentor*, *The Sabbatical Mentor: A Practical Guide to Successful Sabbaticals*.)

The commodification extends to self-help and New Age peddlers. With a DIY folksiness, books like *The Mentor* (Carew, 1999) promise to fill in the mentorship "void" left by the "downsized, restructured business world." And for the esoteric there are "Mentor Spirit Cards" through which the user—by the act of selecting a card out of the pack—will "gain insight into a particular situation or relationship, connect to the wealth of wisdom within, generate clarity and well-being . . . and embody the true spirit of mentorship" (Tyler & Drake, 2014) That sounds easy—I would like some of that!

The longing for and pressure to find just the right mentor, unleashed by the cultural frenzy over the topic is epitomized by the following personal advertisements:

seeking mentor—m4m (*Midtown West*): Just relocated to the city, mid-thirties white business guy looking for a professional and personal mentor. Don't have family or friends here. Been here about a month now but it's been tough to expand my network outside of work. Going through changes after moving and want to grow. I'd like a mentor/older friend to help develop skills, talk to, give advice to, etc. If interested tell me a little about yourself and include a pic if you don't mind. Not opposed to messing around. (Craigslist, New York City, 2017)

Publisher wanted for Mentor/Friendship with Creative Woman w4m (Philadelphia suburbs): I'm a creative SWW, who writes and dabbles with art and who wishes to sit down and do coffee/tea (and to be fascinated and edified thereby) with a publisher. I like, fantasy, adult coloring books, printed visuals, art books, screenplays, metaphysics, more. I may have questions about all of these. I'd like to know about you and your experience. (Craigslist, Philadelphia, Pa., 2017).

Or this ad, as ironically imagined by the writer, David Lazar (1994):

Looking for Mr. Good mentor: Single White Man ISO Mentor, 40–60, tall, non-smoking, into Garcia Marquez, Don Delillo, New Historicism, constructive criticism, monogamy. (p. 26)

Some would swear that the quest for a mentor is best captured satirically—as television shows like the wildly popular and always wry U.S. comedy series, *Seinfeld*, devoted an entire episode to the theme, as did *La La Land*—the BBC sitcom that spoofed on the mentoring foibles that English wannabes endured while trying to make it in Hollywood.

Even though I offer a few over the top examples, my point is that the idea of mentoring has been appropriated extensively even to the point of absurdity. The increasingly widespread attention paid to mentorship is suggestive of many trends but perhaps none more profound than its impact on the *definition of this relationship*. The ubiquity in references to mentoring reflects, reproduces, and expands its already pliant meaning. Mentoring, that is, has become a catch-all word for describing almost any type relation in which any type of advice-giving or support is rendered. This would not be so interesting, nor indeed so problematic, if the idea of mentoring did not carry so much emotional weight. But it does and has for a long time.

Imagos

Tracing a genealogy of mentorship through literary characters and historic archetypes offers us a sketch of mentorship as immensely varied. It becomes clear that there is no one prototype. Indeed, the diverse types of supportive relationships that are connected to the mentor lineage underscore the complexities woven into the foundation of this relation. As summarized in Figure 2.1, variants show that mentorship can be depicted as a relation of learning, power, favors, succession, socialization, adult development, grooming, discipline, community responsibility, occupational stratification, and cultural reproduction. Each of these functions casts the relation with a distinctive emotional tone, yet taken as a whole set the stage for how we imagine and navigate mentoring relationships today.

The oldest reference to Mentor—used as a proper name—is in the ancient Greek text, *The Odyssey* (1996). In his 8th century BC poem, Homer depicts Mentor as a wise, faithful teacher and counselor of Telemachus, son of Odysseus, King of Ithaca. Before setting off for the Trojan Wars, Odysseus instructed Mentor to stay in Ithaca and take full charge of the royal household. Acting as a surrogate, Mentor was given the duty to prepare Telemachus to succeed his father and ascend to the throne. Arguably *the* classic model of a mentor to appear in literature—a paternal figure whose job it was to uphold patriarchal tradition and preserve power—contains ambiguity. Since Mentor appears in the epic poem as Athena—the goddess who sprang from Zeus's head—Mentor is believed to also represent anima or the feminine principle of eros, nurturance, concern for selfhood and risk-taking (Simmons, 1994). It is worth underlining that there is debate about whether our original Mentor is a paternal or maternal figure.

One thing not disputed, however, is that the emotional and moral dependence that the youth has on the mentor figure is substantial. Yet this older person—a non-relative—not father and not mother, but clearly representations of both, retaining boundaries of being outside of the family orbit—becomes enmeshed with the young man with a hefty charge to teach him the ropes of leading a kingdom. How do we grasp this figure who exists outside the family orbit yet becomes so powerful a force in the life of his or her charge? From what paradigm does this come? From early religions?

VARIANTS AND EMOTIONAL CHARACTER OF MENTOR ROLES THROUGHOUT HISTORY		
Primary Mentor Role	Historical Referents	Key Emotional Dynamics
Succession for power/leadership	• *Mentor* in *The Odyssey* • Ancient biblical and religious relationships	Love, respect, dependence, loyalty, admiration, generativity
Grooming for social climbing and elevating social status	• *Mentor* Guidebooks and tutors on social refinement	Love, idealization, dependence, narcissism, shame, control, pride
Protection/Sponsorship for political and material advantage	• Patron/Client relation • Godfather crime father relation	Loyalty, fear, dependence, strategic manipulation, exploitation, control
Technical Training/Discipline to become a respected member of a group	• Master/Apprentice (guilds) • Master/Disciple (spiritual artistic, intellectual)	Control, fear, respect, obedience, dependence
Life Passage Support to transition to adulthood with community blessing	• Rites of passage relations between community elder and youth coming of age	Respect, love, admiration, dependence, community pride

Figure 2.1

Indeed, as the concept of mentoring has grown in popularity over the past forty years, newfound claims are being made regarding its hallowed origins. Arguing that "it is the source of the *term 'mentor'* which lies in Homeric times, not the relationship" (Carruthers, 1993, p. 10), several note that such dyads can be found in the Hebrew Bible (e.g., Moses and Joshua; Elijah and Elisha). This is the central tenet of one book *Mentoring: The Tao of Giving and Receiving Wisdom* (Huang & Lynch, 1995), which traces the birth of mentorship to an ancient eastern tradition in the succession procedures of three Chinese sage kings Yao, Shun, and Yu between 2333 and 2177 BC.

* * *

The next oldest published reference to mentor—used as a noun this time, not a name—appeared in 1851 in a book authored "By a Lady" entitled *The Young Lady's Mentor: A Guide to the Formation of Character. In a Series of Letters to Her Unknown Friends*. Thirty years later another similar guide was written by Alfred Ayres—this one for males—*The Mentor: A Little Book for the Guidance of Such Men and Boys as Would Appear to Advantage in the Society of Persons of the Better Sort* (1884). Both books appropriate the word mentor as a synonym for guidebook on grooming, manners, and character refinement, containing chapters with gender-coded titles like "Ennui, and the desire to be fashionable" and "In public—how to carry an umbrella or cane." Precursors of publications from the self-help industry that would proliferate a century later, these "mentors" or etiquette manuals offered young working class men and women the kind of cultural capital that wealthier peers received from family or finishing school.

> In this world it is only like that seeks like . . . Those who have nothing in common, whose culture and breeding are unlike, whose thoughts are on different things, never seek the society of one another. What points of sympathy are there between the town gallant and the country spark, between the city belle and the dairymaid? If one would be received in the better social circles, one's culture must be of the kind found there, and, above all, one's manners must be marked by the observance of the usages that are to refined social commerce what oil is to the engine. (Ayres, 1884, Prefatory note).

The modern version of this class-based grooming is dramatized theatrically in George Bernard Shaw's Pygmalion (1916) and updated much later in the musical production of My Fair Lady (Lerner & Loewe, 1956). In these performances, mentor Henry Higgins is portrayed as a fussy older British professor who cultivates the scrappy, poor lass, Eliza Doolittle, to act like a proper English lady—by teaching her the King's English, formal dance steps, and deference gestures. Let us not fail to note the diminution in her name.

Mentor in this usage morphs from a term used to describe a guide-book to denote the guide himself. And Henry Higgins and Eliza Doolittle, our mentor–protégé pair become entangled in a teacher–student relationship of cultural makeover. Mentor has knowledge, wisdom, and charitable urges; he takes on protégé Eliza to fix her so she can pass in his well-to-do world. She is his project. And she is beholden to him, yet torn about the assumption around which their relationship turns—the idea that where she comes from, that is, her pedigree is subpar. The relationship is intense, at turns combative and wholly tender. Yet both parties grapple with who they are to each other; confused by strong feelings that go both ways.

* * *

With emphasis on technical training, work obedience, and commercial regulation, a version of mentorship appears during medieval times in the apprentice system associated with guilds. In this arrangement, children as young as ten were apprenticed to elder craftsmen and training under them could extend for up to a dozen years. As the guardian, the master provided bed, food, and sometimes a small salary. Reflecting cultural mores of the time, the master's protection, however, was not in the form of love, but discipline. Apprentices were legally entitled to decent treatment as long as they were industrious and obedient—masters often retained the right to beat reluctant novices. Once completing the training, an apprentice became a journeyman hoping to achieve master status by producing an officially sanctioned *masterpiece*. Reaching beyond the dyadic relation, the apprenticeship system served a gatekeeping function; protecting certain (usually religious) groups from joining the guild—the brotherhood—by excluding others. This version of mentorship was thus as important politically as it was vocationally. Though guilds were abolished several hundred years ago, the exclusionary system—customarily from father to son—continues to operate, keeping out women and minorities in many contemporary trade unions.

* * *

A coercive side of mentorship has traces of the feudal relation between patron landowners or other power holders and "clients" or residents in local communities. Networked extensively to other influential figures, well-positioned with access to resources (e.g., employment, loans, arable land, contracts, bail, licenses, scarce commodities, medicines, scholarships, raw materials and equipment, symbolic credit [e.g., "a good name"], shelter, marriage partners), and prepared to act as an intermediary when protection is needed or red tape needs cutting, the patron grants a wide variety of favors to clients. As he does so, he spins a web of obligation and debt from clients that brings him material return (e.g., domestic service, agricultural labor, tariffs), political support (e.g., votes, campaign aid), and many forms of socio-emotional gratuity (e.g., deference, allegiance, submissiveness, obedience, public shame and humiliation). Located at the interstices of an instrumental orientation associated with concept of an exchange relation ("you scratch my back and I'll scratch yours") yet also bound by the moral and sentimental moorings of interpersonal bonds, Eisenstadt and Roniger (1984) perceptively call attention to the paradoxical features of the patron–client alliance that characterize mentorship as well.

* * *

It seems likely that mentor picks up some of its familial resonance from the special role that uncles have been observed to play in primitive cultures in relation to nephews who are at the cusp of manhood. As personal guide, the uncle is called upon to usher the young man through ceremonial *rites of passage*. In its broad outline, this relation parallels the one between Telemachus and Mentor in *The Odyssey*. The emphasis is on helping youth make the developmental transition to adulthood by learning from the elders to accept the responsibilities involved, facing challenges, and receiving community acknowledgement of one's status as adult (*man*). The dominant sentiment in this mentor–protégé prototype is respect for tradition, discipline, group pride, and honor. In some cultures, this custom extends to girls who are guided by an aunt or other female elder through life transitions. The rituals for females, however, tend not to carry elevation of status in the way that they do for males. Girls simply become women; boys become men and *as men* become community leaders.

* * *

A few other kindred traditions add even more variegation to the mentorship genealogy. Emphasizing protection and loyalty to different genres of fraternity, these include certain types of *Bund* alliances found in the military, godfather relationships in crime families, and deputy–boss relationships found in political circles. Adding to this mix are religious or quasi-religious dyads between spiritual masters and disciples and representations of mentorship that transcend the flesh—among, for example, Native Americans, in the form of spiritual guidance by supernatural forces. There is also a longstanding, yet heretofore underground tradition of sexual mentorship among gay men and lesbians, providing a discreet education and rite of passage to novices.

Inasmuch as a mentorship may have its roots in any or all of these relatively well-defined literary and historical models, it remains a pliable concept. As it has gained currency in recent years, the term has taken on an even greater range of meanings and applications—further expanding its versatility and consequent ambiguity. This stretch is clearly evidenced in everyday usage as well as in academic writings and research.

The "M" word

In the contemporary context, widespread attention paid to mentorship has produced an elastic usage of the term. Mentor has become a buzzword, bandied about generically, and without much thought, to describe almost anyone who even loosely fits the concept including admired teachers and bosses, psychotherapists, sports coaches, literary heroes, parents, spiritual gurus, political figures, and so on. The relaxed usage seems to be based, in part, on a grammatical slip: that is, the word mentor—a noun—has been transfigured into a verb. Like the misnomer of saying that anyone who mothers *is* a mother, our lexicon permits anyone who mentors to be deemed a mentor.

Curiously, while the term seems to be used in an unfettered way in popular culture, in serious conversation about mentorship the opposite seems to hold true. A fair amount of deliberation actually goes into thinking about whether to name a relationship a mentorship. Indeed, as I note earlier, the process of identifying a relationship as a mentorship carries with it a distinct emotional charge. When I ask someone if he or she regards an influential person in his or her life as a "mentor"—specifically using that language—the response is often tentative or qualified. A fair number of people who were clearly uncomfortable with my question clammed up and replied, "it depends on what you mean by mentor." Unclear about how the term should be used, many grope for fixed criteria, wanting *me* to lead in setting the parameters of meaning. Partly this is because the social rules for labeling someone a mentor are not set. In spite of the fact that a good deal of mentorship is "in the eye of the beholden" as David Lazar (1994) facetiously put it—individuals tend to be uneasy about pinning this name to their mentor-like relationships.

This behavior is perplexing but it does provide clues, I think, to anxious feelings that people have about mentoring. Why are people timid about or even averse to using the term? Why would a protégé of a rising star in the creative arts world, for example, describe herself to me as being "receptive to learning *in that particular way*" but quickly add, "*I still hate calling it 'mentoring'*?" And why—at an annual conference for female executives entitled "Building bridges: how to build a powerful network. How to find a mentor. How to be one"—would the keynote speaker say that the term "scares people off?" Robert Coles, esteemed child psychiatrist and author, wondered about this same question as he recalled a somewhat testy exchange about the topic he had had with his own mentor Anna Freud (Coles, 1993):

> . . . "It's a word that is used all the time now, but when I was in college, teaching children in a Boston neighborhood as a volunteer, we never thought of ourselves as mentors or as doing mentoring."
>
> She replied, "Right there you are bringing up something: what does it mean when a word like that becomes part of the consciousness of young volunteers? A mentor traditionally was a revered figure, a trusted and wise adviser, counselor, teacher, a source of guidance and inspiration. That is a lot to ask of a young person! It's a lot to ask of anyone!"
>
> "Are you suggesting that the word becomes a burden?"
>
> "No, not necessarily—but I do think that words have meaning not only in the ordinary sense but in the psychological sense. If I am a mentor, and if others are asked to think of me as a mentor, and if I think of myself as a mentor, then people like you and me, whose business it is to take notice of what the mind does under various circumstances, should—well, do just that!"

... "I hadn't thought of the word "mentor" as a term that would provoke a special variety of expectations (and perhaps, subsequently, disappointments) in those who are mentored. I had regarded the word from the social and cultural angle rather than the psychological one." (pp. 96–97)

Perhaps the act of naming can seem daring as it announces something about the identity of a relationship that may be called into question by the other party. What if, frets the junior colleague, my boss who I so highly regard doesn't think of himself as my mentor? What if he doesn't think of us as having such a special relationship? Questions about reciprocity in the naming process can stir up a fair amount of anxiety. I have seen this and it can be quite painful. I can recall one man, for instance—an environmental scientist turned career management expert who had been involved with his mentor for thirty years—was nervous to let me call his mentor to be a part of my study. After peeling away at the layers of his concern, it seemed that he did not want to find out that his glowing feelings for the mentor were not returned—he was afraid of finding out that the mentor did not see himself in such an important, caring role. The pattern can go the other way too—sometimes it is the senior person sees him or herself in the mentor role but this is not recognized by the would-be protégé. As such misnomers occur, one risks exposure and humiliation by overstating the level of intimacy, commitment, and significance of a relationship by using a terminology that may be unrequited.

This dynamic is searingly dramatized in Yasmina Reza's well received play *Art* (1996) in which two middle-aged men—longtime friends—spend an evening together arguing over the fact that one of them, Serge, has spent an enormous sum of money to purchase an all-white (that is, blank) painting. Misapprehensions about the nature of the friendship are caustically revealed as Marc—the one most unnerved by his friend's new love and appreciation for cutting edge art—confesses what he had always assumed to be the core understanding upon which the friendship was based ... a mentorship. In this mortifying exchange, he learns from his would-be protégé, Serge, that this was not a mutual perspective.

MARC: In my time, you'd never have bought that picture.

SERGE: What's that supposed to mean, *"In your time?"*

MARC: The time you made a distinction between me and other people, when you judged things by *my* standards.

SERGE: Was there such a time?

MARC: That's just cruel. And petty.

SERGE: No, I assure you, I'm staggered.

MARC: . . . There was a time you were proud to be my friend . . . You congratulated yourself on my peculiarity, on my taste for standing apart. You enjoyed exhibiting me untamed to your circle, you, whose life was so normal. I was your alibi. But . . . eventually . . . that sort of affection dries up . . . Belatedly, you claim your independence.

SERGE: "Belatedly" is nice.

MARC: But I detest your independence. It's violence. You've abandoned me. I've been betrayed. As far as I'm concerned, you're a traitor.

Silence

SERGE: . . . *If I understand correctly, [you were] my mentor? . . . And if I loved you as my mentor . . . what was the nature of your feelings?* (italics added)

MARC: You can guess.

SERGE: Yes, yes, but I want to hear you say it.

MARC: I enjoyed your admiration. I was flattered. I was always grateful to you for thinking of me as a man apart. I even thought being a man apart was a somehow superior condition, until one day you pointed out to me that it wasn't.

SERGE: This is very alarming.

MARC: It's the truth . . . .

SERGE: I had no idea whatsoever—really, it's come as a complete surprise—the extent to which I was under your influence and in your control.

MARC: Not in my control, as it turns out . . . (pp. 51–53)

Conversations about naming, including whether and when to use the "M word"—as one banker I interviewed put it—are among the most revealing discussions I have had in my research as they point to fears and fantasies about power, control, idealization, loyalty, obligation, dependence, merger, and generativity. How each person interprets and applies the terms of mentorship brings to light some of the underlying wishes and conflicts they import into these alliances. Talk about the word mentor, put simply, stimulates deeper reflection on the psychodynamics of such relationships in one's life.

Early in his relationship with Frank Conroy, novelist Tom Grimes (2010) notes in his loving tribute, *Mentor: A Memoir*, that he fretted about how to think about and name the connection and feelings he was having towards Frank. As his student at the Iowa Writer's Workshop, Tom was thrown into a tizzy when Frank—quite aware of Tom's interest in writing a novel about baseball—invited him to his home to watch the World Series game:

> I couldn't decide if he was my teacher, mentor, friend, father, or a composite of these figures . . . My problem is that I didn't know who to be in my relationship with Frank . . . Deepening our relationship, though, meant I had a greater chance of being rejected by him if I let him down in any way . . .

Agonizing about the ambiguity, taking great pains to make sure that boundaries were not crossed or ignored, he wrote to Frank,

> Frank, I don't know what to say about your invitation, other than thanks. I have to admit, though, I'm not sure where the line between teacher and friend lies, and I don't want to appear too eager to cross it, or too indifferent not to cross it. I also don't want to complicate my writing or your reading of my novel. Your critical voice already dominates my thoughts as I write. And while it would be one thing for my work to disappoint you as a teacher, it would be another matter to disappoint you as a friend. I hope you understand my confusion. Please don't interpret it as a lack of gratitude. What I feel is the exact opposite. If I didn't, I wouldn't have written this letter. Sincerely, Tom (pp. 33–34).

For some, naming oneself a mentor implies self-aggrandizement, a puffing up of one's influence on another person. One protégé—a forty-something year old woman in advertising—described her supervisor as "embarrassed that he even thought of himself as a mentor."

Although it became clear during our interview that the mentor was not only comfortable enacting the role of teacher, role model, and sponsor—he was actually a staunch actor in each of these mentoring roles—he just did not like to admit this. Laced with Midwestern reserve, he distanced himself from the title of mentor because it conveyed an air of self-importance, a kind of hubris, a social taboo from where he came.

In other cases, mentors shy away from the title because they're afraid of getting caught up in long term obligation. Signaling tension, a junior faculty member in the Asian Studies department at an elite university noted that her mentor's "first reaction [to participating in my study] was '*are* we in a mentor relationship?' " Indeed, playing down her effect on the protégé was part of what made the mentor "an attractive person—she does not know her own power . . . or charisma." Curiously, I found this otherwise intrepid senior professor anxious at the mere suggestion that she could wield such intense influence over others. Somewhat withholding as a mentor, she drew boundaries constantly to buffer herself from the neediness of the protégé learner, afraid, I thought, of the possibility of quashing her younger colleague with her potent intellect and courageous academic positions. Still, this mentor's even greater anxiety had to do with dependence. She worried that making any gestures that would amplify the significance of the relationship (e.g., openly acknowledging it *as a mentorship*) might be read by the protégé as an invitation to maintain a lifetime connection to her. She did not want the strings attached—to her, mentorship represented a slippery slope to engulfment.

Concerns about boundary maintenance also were prominent in discussions with another mentor pair—both performing artists. Though claiming "I don't really call myself her mentor," this leader in experimental dance conceded that the term was palatable *only* if the counterpart term was *"not protégé."* "Protégé to me," she explained, "means formed in one's own image . . . [implying] a degree of investment on the part of the older person that's not healthy—that their sense of self-esteem and ego gratification [are] bound up in the achievement of the younger person." Going on to render the mentor–protégé dyad as "creepy" gave me a vivid imago of this woman's queasiness about mentorship merger. The idea that a disciple would be unable to separate herself from her mentor's persona and, as the corollary, that the mentor's narcissistic pleasures would vicariously hinge on the disciple's success seemed inevitable, if not discursively managed. The word could not be separated from the reality.

Some reject the title of mentor altogether. In a brutally honest essay about his terror of mentorship, Phillip Lopate (1994) wrote:

> How do I reconcile my skepticism about mentorship . . . Partly, I think, by denying the degree to which I may actually play the role of mentor. I often "pretend" not to see the embarrassing extent to which a student is in my thrall; or I try to defuse the situation with humor and impersonality, while continuing to offer concrete assistance. I have had students pursue me with requests for recommendations, blurbs, advice, twenty years or more after they studied with me; some are shamelessly using me, true, but a few may actually think of me as their mentor. Yet I have refused the intimacy of the term in my own mind. (pp. 110–111)

While many are put off by the emotional burdens they read into the terms mentor and protégé, some are ready and willing to seize on these words for their seductive potential. Fantasies of control and professional ascendancy seem to give license to shallow use of these words as a way to engineer adulation, compliance, and productivity from would-be protégés. This is particularly striking in the case of a mid-level manager at a pharmaceutical firm who only a few weeks after meeting her assistant, Paz, announced that she would "*be* her mentor." Simply calling the relationship a mentorship—a naming by fiat, however, did not make it one.

> *Bonnie:* Did you think of her in terms of being a mentor? Would you have called her that?
>
> *Paz:* . . . *She* used it early on . . . Shortly after I started working for her she started to say, "I'm kind of mentoring you." . . . Later on she had explained something to me and I think I said something back like, "You've taught me so much as a mentor." I didn't mean it in any . . . like . . . trying to kiss butt way or anything. She goes "Oh you've just given me goosebumps," like she felt "so moooved by that." (Paz purses her lips to make a cow face as she elongates the word "move" as if to suggest a note of mockery in response to her mentor's sentimentality.) And . . . I guess like from that, evolved this relationship.

Paz confided to me that it took her a good year before she felt it fitting to think of or call her boss—a mentor. She could not make this attribution unless she felt it genuinely. When she finally did use the term, it was conveyed as an emotional gift, similar to the sentiment expressed by a daughter-in-law who takes the leap to call her spouse's mother, "mum."

These illustrations highlight the fact that naming a mentorship—whatever emotional associations the term conjures up—is viewed as a declaration of commitment to perceiving the relationship in a particular cast as opposed to having it remain in a nominal limbo. Yet, there are no markers for deciding at what point a relation moves from a garden variety professional or personal relationship into a mentorship. Parties might recognize the existence of a special bond but feel unclear about what language to use to describe this quality. A useful analogy is the dating couple who grapple with whether to think about and refer to one another as "friends," "lovers," or "significant others" and when to make shifts in attribution from one to another. However arbitrary, each naming creates a frame for the relation and as such becomes part of it discursive construction—reflecting and shaping how partners orient themselves towards each other. Stephen Duck (1995) got this right when he wrote, "[t]he existence of a relationship is at least partly (but importantly), a result of a certain set of people coming to agree that there is one . . . [O]nce partners come not only to believe that they are in a certain sort of relationship but to discuss and share that belief, then their discourse alters correspondingly" (p. 537). In the case of mentorship, not only does their talk change, so does their concept of the emotional connection. While it articulates a more explicit outline for the relationship, using the "M word" clearly saddles parties with expectations and responsibilities, and an infusion of conscious and unconscious psychic fantasies, longings, and anxieties.

Academic splitting

Regrettably, looking to academic literature is not terribly helpful if one wishes to nail down a consistent definition of mentorship. Indeed, most who study mentorship agree that there is little consensus about what goes on in such relationships. Rather than trying to grasp the diverse strands of such relationships, scholars from disparate fields tend to use the narrow lens of their disciplines to dictate what they investigate. Generally speaking, while organizational and management scholars take a utilitarian view of mentorship as a strategic career building alliance, sociologists see the relation as a political liaison and gate-keeping system whose goal is to elevate some groups while limiting access to advancement for others. And while scholars coming from the cluster of fields dealing with youth and adult development see mentorship as a vehicle for promoting socialization and life-long learning for adaptive self-enhancement, psychoanalytical researchers are most interested in and draw out the connections between mentorship, inner life, and childhood experience to gain insight about unconscious strivings and emotionally repetitive themes in adult relations. This leaves the view of mentorship as a route to community membership and civic participation to anthropologists and social workers, linking individuals to group and cultural legacies. Although each provides insight about one area of mentorship, rarely do researchers from any of these fields move away from their disciplinary myopia to consider a full picture of mentorship. This fragmentation comes at great expense to our comprehension of what is going on in mentorship. By failing to grasp the various strands of mentorship, researchers sidestep fundamental ambiguities in the relationship. Consequently, tensions between utilitarian, political, developmental, transferential, communal, and cultural strivings are practically invisible in academic research on mentorship, even though they are clearly embodied and enacted in lived relationships.

Another rift among scholars—beyond the substantive focus of what one studies—deals with how we envision the relational structure of a mentorship and whether we believe that this perspective is even worthy of consideration. On this, two divergent conceptions have emerged—one that cares about relational structure and one that does not. I label these the *classic* and *functional* approaches, respectively, to mentorship.

First and the more traditional approach of the two, the classic one regards mentorship as a *distinct type of authority relation*. Mentor is envisioned as an older, more experienced person who helps a younger person learn to navigate in the adult world and world of work. Mentor can be an immediate supervisor, a former boss, someone within an organization but outside of the direct line of authority, or a person outside of one's organization—a veteran professional in the same field as a protégé.

Classic mentorship is understood to be initiated and sustained informally. It does not appear on an organizational chart, it is not institutionalized, nor does it have official status in the sense that no formal role responsibilities are attached to it. Mentor and protégé may strike up the relationship while working together on a project, they may be introduced by colleagues or friends, or they may meet within the context of professional associations and networks. Institutional mentoring programs are rarely designed to create classic mentorships when they pair people to work together in a mentoring alliance—yet over time, a classic type of relation may evolve.

Classic mentorships often grow to be quite emotionally intense and intimate. Well documented examples of classic pairs abound in public life. Think of Steve Jobs, founder and former CEO of Apple and his social media genius protégé, Mark Zuckerberg of Facebook. Include here also Freud and his deep psychology mentorship of Jung, as well as the so-called "attack dog" defense attorney Roy Cohn's street fighter mentorship of the then real estate mogul, Donald Trump. In most instances, classic relationships are platonic but occasionally the pair become lovers. This is the case in the mentorship–cum–sexual liaison between Nazi sympathizing philosopher Martin Heidegger and his anti-fascist student–lover–comrade intellectual Hannah Arendt, whose stormy mentorship—referred to later in this book—is heart wrenchingly portrayed in Elzbieta Ettinger's biography (1995). Making headlines in the news not so long ago was the affair and betrayal of state secrets between David Petraeus, former U.S. C.I.A. Director and his biographer-protégé and military intelligence officer, Paula Broadwell. Although there are histrionics in all of the above relationships owing to their fame, or infamy, as it were, they all fit the classic model. Feeling a fierce bond, parties in classic mentorships are (or become) cognizant of reciprocal obligations, mutual gratifications, and the risks and benefits that go with the relationship. While such relationships usually take time to develop and can last throughout a person's life, breakups along the way can be acrimonious and cause great pain.

Daniel Levinson, mentioned earlier, was one of the first to profile classic mentorship in *The Seasons of a Man's Life* (Levinson et al., 1978). Despite grappling for words to capture the essence of the mentor–protégé relation, Levinson clearly saw it as having unique properties,

No word currently in use is adequate to convey the nature of the relationship we have in mind here. Words such as "counselor" and "guru" suggest the subtler meanings, but they have other connotations that would be misleading. The term mentor is generally used in a much narrower sense to mean teacher, advisor or sponsor. As we use the term, it means all these things and more (p. 97).

Hence, classic mentorships are understood to contain elements of other types of advisory and support relationships—but their gestalt, so to speak, is seen as qualitatively different from and greater than the sum total of those parts.

This proposition—that *classic mentorship assumes a form that is different from and greater than the sum total of its parts*—is crucial. It stands in marked contrast to the *functional* approach to mentorship—a view that concentrates on the parts themselves. Rather than frame the mentor–protégé relationship as a unique type of social relationship, consultants and researchers who adopt the functional view see mentoring in terms of career and psychosocial assistance—frequently referred to as "developmental functions" (Kram, 1988)—carried out in support relationships. From within this paradigm, it does not matter who performs these activities—either peers, or superiors, or friends, or relatives can do the mentoring. Nor does it matter whether one or many types of help are offered. How long the help is offered over time is also not important. What *is* important is that some type of mentoring activity is carried out by someone to help another develop professionally. Hence, while classic mentorship focuses on who the mentor and protégé *are in relation* to each other, the functional focus on what mentor and protégé *do*.

It would be hard to deny that the functional concept mirrors the widespread and lax use of the term mentoring in the broader culture. There tends to be a no strings attached quality to functional mentorship. And the authority foundation of the relationship seems to be optional. Anyone can do it for however long they like. It is not hard to see why this is appealing. And yet with a stroke of an academic pen (or keyboard) the relational structure of mentorship is vanquished; and with that goes its emotional complexity. Part of the impetus for writing this book is to try to preserve (or resurrect) the integrity of that structure so we do not lose the framework through which to detect the emotional messiness of mentorship. Let me put this another way: just as friendship consists of more than friendly and generous behavior and motherhood involves more than acts of mothering and nurturance, *mentorship needs to be seen as more than a skin deep enactment of mentoring functions*. Otherwise, as cautioned earlier, just as the noun mentor has been permitted to collapse into the verb, so it may come to be that the unique and profoundly influential relational form of mentorship—at least theoretically—may be dissolved by its contents.

A working conception

I have tried to convince the reader in this chapter that any attempt to define or conceptualize mentorship must start with the premise that it is an intrinsically ambiguous social relation. The scripts of mentor and protégé are etched with emotionally powerful expectations, hopes, and anxieties as well as an array of historical archetypes and contemporary exhortations that offer mixed messages as to what is supposed to occur and how mentor and protégé are supposed to behave in the relationship. And if one has taken to reading mainstream or scholarly texts to gain a better handle on how to think about mentorship, the relation only seems more elusive. Academics, organizational researchers, management experts, and authors in the popular press not only do not agree on how to get a handle on the topic but by continually reifying it—as a *thing to have*—they tend to blot out some of mentorship's most important relational strengths and vulnerabilities.

So, where does this leave us? As I have explained in the introductory chapter, I adopt a dialectical approach in order to be able to hold the tensions in mentorship, placing them in the forefront of analyses. Rather than devalue or hide the tensions, I define mentorship as an emotionally-bonded, intrinsically ambivalent authority relation whose primary functions are developmental. Hence, I am just as interested in exploring who mentor and protégé are in their relation to one another, as I am in what mentors and protégés "do" in the relationship. To me, these are inseparable: how much and what types of guidance are provided is indelibly shaped by the character and dynamics of the relationship. Mentoring can, that is, revolve around career, vocational, adult development, socialization, political, or cultural grooming aims but whatever the content, it is fundamentally a relation of authority. Without theorizing mentorship as a relation of authority, it loses a mainstay of its emotional hold and source of its ambivalence. The next chapter delves into the emotional tensions as they emerge in the process of idealization between mentors and protégés.

CHAPTER THREE

Walking on water with feet of clay: idealization in mentorship

Mentorship arouses idealization. It is built to do so. And within bounds, the process of putting another on a pedestal to admire and emulate is beneficial. "When we idealize others," writes Ruthellen Josselson (1996), "we locate in them qualities that we wish to own for ourselves . . . our longing is toward possession of that which is outside of ourselves that appears far grander than what we know ourselves to be" (p. 127). Possibility, that is, is the oxygen of idealization. Still, as in most relationships of any intensity, idealization in mentorship is complicated and inherently problematic, usually leading to a fall from grace for the mentor and inner turmoil and disappointment for the protégé. But let us put aside the conflicts that come with idealization to look more closely first at its benefits for mentoring relationships.

Perfection, omnipotence, magic

Idealization allows the protégé to look towards a mentor with admiration and hope. Its potency lies in the ways the self imagines becoming greater, enhanced, and more perfect or powerful through linking oneself to the idealized other. Often mentors and protégés will use the word "chemistry" to label the mix of attraction, excitement, identification, and goodness of fit that are the base of idealization. This loving, marveling stance—most intense in the earlier phase of the relationship—is an emotionally bonding experience and provides a powerful lubricant for the processes of learning, maturation, and influence that will unfold.

For some protégés, the idealized mentor appears to be extraordinary, embodying the image of perfection and the hope that one may attain that quality for him or herself. Perfection may be perceived in the mentor's talents at carrying out work, knowledge of the field, skill mastery, deftness at handling organizational relationships and colleagues, success at balancing work and family, etc. Perfection may also be read into the mentor's personal qualities: interpersonal style, mental faculties, personality, integrity, ethics, values, confidence, life wisdom, physical appearance, vibe, etc. As spoken by three protégés:

> *Patricia*: I adored her and wanted to be just like her . . . I also did have a little hero worship because she was just so smart, and quick, and effervescent, and energetic, and took such control!

> *Paul*: He is brilliant—some would call him a polymath because the scope of his knowledge seems limitless. And he has a wiz of a memory . . . if only I could be like him . . .

> *Pamela*: (giggling) She looked really cool and hip . . . wearing a black leather jacket. It was my first San Francisco experience in quite a while. And I was this little Iowan . . . I felt "she's so hip!" *My own* clothes were kind of dorky. So I was like, "I don't know if I can work with you cause I just don't think I'd be cool enough!"

Sometimes the idealization is based on a projection backwards in time such as when a protégé imputes an aspect of greatness to the mentor's life in the past. One protégé, for example, hailed her mentor as a courageous and committed activist during the sixties anti-war and civil rights movements in the U.S.—deifying him as "just shy of godliness."

Not surprisingly, the fact that mentor and protégé are in an authority relation both feeds and amplifies the emotional hierarchy that frames idealization. Not only does it trigger transference reactions—evoking childhood fantasies of connection with parental perfection—

it also adds other layers of feeling to the mix. In other words, the same perfect qualities that give rise to hope may also inspire fear. This has been shown to be a healthy fear, however, as it contains a blend of trepidation and challenge that characterizes good authority in mentorship (Sennett, 1980). Bowled over by her mentor, one protégé—a midlevel manager at a large publishing company—reflected thoughtfully about what many others have summed up as "fear and revere:"

> *Paulina*: I found her extremely imposing at first . . . very formidable. I *still* find her very formidable, actually. That aspect hasn't changed . . . but my reaction to it has . . . In the first year of our relationship I think she called me a couple of times to set up meetings and I'd hear this deep gravelly voice on the other end of the phone and I'd almost jump and put the receiver down!

Yet, Paulina notes that this same panic is part of what drove her to take risks:

> *Paulina*: "Intimidating," "intense," "high voltage," are words that I've heard people use to describe her . . .

> *Bonnie*: But there are different reads on all of these terms. They could be sources of idealization—of looking up to somebody—or they could be powerfully frightening.

> *Paulina*: I think they have both effects, actually. When I worked on my first project with her I was sort of exhilarated and also felt very exposed, and very put on the spot, and very vulnerable at the same time. And it was definitely giving sparks off. It was really helpful in terms of my being creative, and challenged, and stretched to come up with answers. And that was great. But I just had this feeling that the stakes were tremendously high for either coming up with the wrong answer or not having thought through something enough. In fact I learned to react much more quickly than I had before or at least to react verbally. I would have an initial reaction but I would filter it through any number of layers of qualms and qualifications before anything would ever come out of my mouth. And in working with Marsha, I've become much more willing to volunteer something, even if it isn't the right answer even though I may get sat on for it.

So, what is the fear about? In one sense, it comes from the wish to please. Idealization stirs up wishes to be *good for* the mentor (proving one is worthy of mentor's notice and affection) and *as good as* the mentor (striving to be like the mentor). When the relationship is going well, the attendant fear—a form of nervous excitement—serves as a stimulus to try hard, apply oneself, prove oneself, experience affirmation, and gain approval. Of course, the fear also comes from the threat of disapprobation. We hear these themes in the backbeat of anxiety that drives Paulina's efforts to get past her own typical obsessiveness in order to show that she can be more decisive—in other words, to be more like her mentor in order to please her mentor. At least nascently aware of the vulnerability built into the relationship, the adoring protégé is afraid of rejection.

Idealization also links to power—both fantasized and real. A protégé who views the mentor as larger than life—a towering figure who can make things happen, set agendas, marshal resources, mingle with other prominent people, etc., may feel thrilled and emboldened by being associated to that power. Psychoanalytically speaking, we are dealing again with a transference reaction here stemming from an understanding that idealization awakens early wishes in the protégé to merge with an omnipotent parent. Tom Grimes offers a delicious example of this in his memoir. As he listened to his mentor, Frank Conroy, go on about William Faulkner as if Faulkner, the great American novelist, was someone who lived down the street and, as if Faulkner and his mentor were intimate friends, Grimes seemed tickled. In Conroy's presence, Grimes felt closer to greatness as he imagined himself as being linked (by association) to a literary star. Talk about feeling enlarged!

In her pioneering book *Men and Women of the Corporation* (1977), organizational sociologist, Rosabeth Moss Kanter, reminds us that real power (i.e., not just in one's mind) may come to the protégé who is allied with a powerful mentor. There is much evidence that protégés are seen as extensions of influential mentors and as such receive social credit from them in the form of "reflected power." Such vicarious power comes with symbolic and material rewards such as reputational boosts and other organizational or professional perks including invitations to high-level meetings or social events otherwise reserved for executives in a company's inner circle.

* * *

Building on fantasies of perfection and power is the mentor believed to be endowed with superhuman gifts. Protégés may be inspired by the notion that mentors possess some ultimate truth or kernel of essential wisdom that gives their opinions the weight of gospel. This helps explain why protégés will admit to "hanging on to every word" of a mentor, hearing suggestions as commands or exhortations, dissecting feedback for shades of hidden meaning, and feeling compelled to justify their own decisions meticulously in light of a mentor's advice. They do so—as we hear in the words of these three protégés—out of regard for their mentors as a kind of seer or guru:

> *Penny*: I am constantly dazzled by Michael's mind. He's a genius in how he thinks about our projects . . . although I'm embarrassed to admit it, I sometimes feel I'd like to sit at his feet (!)

> *Prana*: Marta is just one unbelievably smart cookie. She sees beyond any kind of sham. She's just—she's brilliant. She's very frightening that way.

> *Paloma*: I think of Mark as a wizard . . . He's very in tune with people, very in touch with the human condition, and a very wise person. *I'm* just this kid with moss behind my ears.

In nearly identical words, two protégés alluded to the sway of their mentor's opinions on their own thought processes as they tried to make decisions:

> *Peter*: When Marina says something, I listen to it really hard and I only disagree with it if I can come up with enough intellectual justification to counter it . . . So, for example, it was really hard for me to decide to take an unpaid leave even though I know financially we could never afford it. But [because Marina was the one who suggested it] I still had to kind of go through my justifications really carefully and make sure that I was thinking about it *the right way*.

> *Paulina*: I guess because Marsha gives me some kind of friendly advice or a nudge in a certain direction, I tend to take it much more seriously than I would if it was advice given to me by either someone my own age or someone that wasn't in this position . . . It's weightier. And usually I have a stronger reaction to it whether it's one way or the other. If I'm not going to abide by it, I usually try to justify that. Where with somebody else I might just say "Okay . . ." and not exactly dismiss it but not feel bound to react to it in some way.

Acknowledging the weight of her own influence, one mentor at an international media company seemed to relish the thought that she played a god-like role with her protégé—perhaps even more so than she was aware of—hinted at in her slip in speech:

> *Michaela*: [Mentoring] plays out in a very simple way . . . You make your vision very well *divined* (pause) . . . *defined*. And you choose people that can accept it.

Although mentors tend not to be so cognizant of the prophetic force of their words and actions, one mentor sensed that her protégé saw her as holding the key to secret knowledge that, if divulged, could instantly and magically make *her* wise too:

> *Maddy*: I think Padma feels like there's something I know that she would like to know . . . *some secret*, you know, *some something*. But the fact is that it's kind of experiential. You can't impart it because you learn it from experience.

Noting that the *something* that the mentor possesses comes from experience and not from a mysterious secret leads us to a second key point about idealizing the mentor as a magical figure. This has to do with a belief that the mentor has attained ideal qualities because he or she is *endowed* with them. I have heard many protégés describe their mentors as innately exceptional, for example, in having "amazing intuition," "the patience of a saint," or "godly" in possessing vast knowledge. This inclination to view the mentor as superhuman seems to provide the protégé with a hypothesis—although usually a not so conscious one—about how a mentor has come to be as wondrous, perfect, and powerful as he or she appears to be and that is: *effortlessly*. Through this lens, it appears to the protégé that the mentor has not had to work hard to become so accomplished and that his or her process of development has been struggle-free. As I will describe later in this chapter, while a "magical mentor fantasy" can have magnetic pull—drawing the protégé to the mentor in the hope of being anointed by his or her imprint and good grace—it can also back-fire by impeding the developmental process. We will return to this point.

Though I mainly deal in this chapter with the protégé's idealiza-tion of the mentor, one should note that mentors may also idealize protégés—seeing in them an image of the perfect son or daughter or, perhaps, a younger version of themselves or someone they would have wished to have been like. Like progeny, the idealized protégé can seem to hold the promise of fulfilling the mentor's own unrealized dreams and in this sense can serve as a rueful reminder of what might have been. About her protégé, for example, one mentor commented:

> *Margaret*: One thing I admire about Pat is that she's developing a career one step at a time and being pretty thoughtful about each step. It's always that she's building something . . . I mean I think she's *so* unlike me in a way . . . When I look at Pat, I think, "if I could have just been like her."

The idealized protégé also embodies the possibility that the mentor's knowledge, values, worldview, etc. will be carried on into the future. For the mentor, idealization tends to be bound up with generativity wishes examined later in the book.

The ego ideal

I want to pause here to take up the question of *why we idealize* and examine why this dynamic crops up so consistently and with such vigor in mentorship.

Psychoanalytic theories of various persuasions offer explanations about the fantasies, emotional strivings, and transference reactions that give rise to and result from seeing another person as perfect, magical, and omnipotent. They help us understand why such feelings can be so intense and persistent even when they are, by all conventional standards, inappropriate, strategically unwise, or seemingly irrational. Why, for example, do some individuals get caught up in a torrent of idealization with mentors who are distant, withholding, uninterested, or highly narcissistic?

Psychoanalysis has its most robust conception of idealization in the notion of the *ego ideal*, written about extensively by the French psychoanalyst Janine Chasseguet-Smirgel (1985). According to the theory of the ego ideal, a person projects on to parents first, and then on to other authority figures later on, an ideal conception of the self otherwise known as the ego ideal. The ego ideal is believed to originate during early infancy at the dawning recognition of human limitation and dependence. Psychically, it serves as a representation of hope for return to "lost paradise"—a wondrous state of complete love and power. Relationships with authority figures such as mentors—on to whom one may transfer parental imagos—rekindle the prospect that one may regain a lost state of perfection—that in which one was his or her own ideal. A mentor serves as a beacon of hope that the protégé can attain his or her own sense of mastery and edge towards the ideal. Chasseguet-Smirgel aptly refers to this aspect of the ego ideal's function as a "maturation drive" (p. 44).

The ego ideal for an aspiring jazz cellist named Portia—as projected on to her mentor, Maura—is described as something "solid:"

> Portia: I was wowed because . . . I just expected it to be kind of a work-ing relationship. I guess maybe I never really had a true mentor. I don't even know exactly what that means. But it was so special . . . I just feel that it's inspiration. It's being able to have some sort of solid thing that you can hope to attain or something.
>
> Bonnie: What is that thing? Is it something that she represents?

Portia gushes as she goes on to describe that something:

> Portia: To me she represents being able to be . . . a happy, centered, great person . . . I mean she's created a life for herself that she's proud of and happy with. And I don't see that very often . . . And I think that's defi-nitely the most important thing that I'd like. I don't have that now but that's what I'm hoping to attain . . . On some very core level she has created something that means something to her and to the people around her. She's done remarkable things especially in her improvisa-tional pieces . . . She's been featured in the Chicago New Music Review . . . and Bruce Andrews writes about her! She's managed to get out there and touch people that maybe wouldn't be affected by free jazz . . . The friends and contacts she has are phenomenal . . . So definitely the most important thing is to see what she's created, how she's created her life and to know that it's possible to create your life in a way that you can feel good about and be proud of.
>
> Bonnie: She represents some set of possibilities?
>
> Portia: Yes, definitely, definitely . . . It's like a light. No matter what's going on . . . it's like this glowing ball of bright possibilities.

While Portia says that Maura provides her with something "solid," she goes on to describe it paradoxically, as a "glowing ball of bright possibilities." Her mentor, that is, offers her solid light—a buoyant source of energy and hope that has the feel of something substantial and anchoring. This captures beautifully the guiding yet ethereal quality of the ego ideal.

Illusion, enactment, reality

While serving as a mode of attachment between mentor and protégé—infusing the relation with eros and fostering the processes of learning and development—idealization evokes defensive reactions such as regression in the service of the ego. That is, the process calls up infantile wishes and fantasies in which the self undergoes a temporary loss of ego functioning. Judgment, for instance, is off kilter since idealization entails projection and distortion—an observation underscored by Freud (1914c) in his definition of idealization as a "process that concerns the object; by it that object without any alteration in its nature, is aggrandized and exalted in the subject's mind" (p. 94).

Other defenses associated with idealization are splitting and denial. The illusion of the mentor's greatness is partly a way to keep negative feelings at bay, in other words. Several psychoanalytic writers have emphasized the defensive use of idealization as a way to avoid anxiety or other unwanted affects. This was the crux of Melanie Klein's (1986[1946]) formulation of "splitting"—a defense mechanism in which "bad" feelings are believed to be evacuated from consciousness, allowing only "good" affects to be felt or mentalized. Klein's theory is that splitting is a primitive defense mechanism stemming from infancy when the baby, in order to protect an image of the mother (aka "the breast") as all-good, disavows her hateful feelings towards the mother. This is necessary to insure psychic survival lest persecutory fantasies run amok. The result, Klein would suggest, is that there is a trace of defensive idealization in us throughout life—triggered to avoid the pain of disappointment in the other's shortcomings and in not being able to control the other. This manifests as a defensive refusal to recognize those limitations.

I want to underline at this point that the ambivalence and defensive maneuvering that attends idealization in mentorship are not necessarily or even usually consciously experienced. At its libidinal peak, idealizing feelings can feel like a mad crush. It should not be too surprising, therefore, that one might try to protect his or her starry-eyed view of the mentor. The image of the perfect, magical, and all-powerful mentor casts him or her as a potential savior. Baum (1992) wrote about this, describing protégés' hope that under the watch of a mentor, they would be sheltered from the aggressive demands and inequitable realities of organizational and professional life. In Baum's words, idealization helps protégés:

> . . . defend against the dangers of organizational life and to transform the organization into a place where work and advancement are safe . . . Libidinal caring replaces the vision of an organization in which aggression (expressed in competition and embodied in hierarchical distinctions) rules . . . Thinking of an organization in these terms transforms it from an economic enterprise into a family, where appeals to trust and loyalty supplant concerns about fairness of the division of labor and profit (p. 227).

In addition to the defensive functions of idealization, one should keep in mind that the fantasies animating idealization are not static. Their content is fluid and changeable, and the role that they play in organizing and coloring a protégé's perception of the mentor can intensify and weaken. Particularly as relationships evolve and mature over time, a protégé's susceptibility to idealize wanes, giving way to more realistic appraisals of the mentor's talents and abilities, expectations, and flaws. The ebbs and flow of idealization and its corollary, deidealization, will be explored in depth later in this chapter.

Also important is the fact that idealization does not necessarily find direct expression nor is it always observable. While excessive praise, fawning, compulsive obedience or acquiescence, constant solicitations for approval, and outward signs of the desire to please can be read as pretty obvious signs of idealization, most times, it is expressed in more subtle ways. One protégé, Paola—a junior professor of English literature—told me a story, for example, that called attention to the fact that idealization is often acted out rather than verbalized. Once when her mentor was giving a paper at a conference overseas, Paola found herself spending more time than was usual or necessary to fulfill her research assistant hours in her mentor's office. She found herself somewhat "lost in time" as she carefully browsed through his library. Staggered by the scope of the mentor's knowledge (in her idealizing stance, she assumed he had read every book), Paola told me that she'd leafed through dozens of books to try to figure out what *she* would need to read to ascend to her mentor's league. Such an enactment—touching the books, glancing furtively at many of them as if trying to establish a connection to her mentor, etc.—had all the signs of an idealizing protégé wowed by an epic sense of her mentor's intellectual prowess while trying to get some of that to rub off on her.

Finally, it is important to point out that while the process of idealization blossoms in fantasy, some people are more idealizable than others. That is to say, fantasy constructions are usually based on some actual attributes of the other. Certainly the amount of power and prestige that a mentor has in an organization or field are important factors. And the mentor's personal charisma obviously feeds the process as well. In the extreme, we hear the terms Svengali or guru applied to the hypnotic lure of a captivating mentor. At the same time, mentors who are less well regarded in their fields or careers, or who are struggling with their own insecurities about professional adequacy may not become objects of idealization in the same way as mentors who exude and feel confidence in their work and professional stature. All told, while there are broad trends in how idealization plays out in mentorship, there are many individual, dyadic, organizational, and occupational particularities that must be kept in mind when analyzing this dynamic in any given relationship.

Vulnerability

Up to this point in the chapter, we have looked at the longings and aspirations that fuel idealization as a more or less positive force and bonding agent in mentorship. Still, core to the perspective I wish to advance is recognizing and making sense of the ambivalence that is intrinsic to this process. Already we have identified ambivalence in the mixed feelings of fear and awe that protégés experience as they look up to mentors in ways that encourage them to want to rise to that level. This just begins to scratch the surface. Idealization engenders many other kinds of difficult feelings and tensions. These can impede or help the mentoring process depending on how such feelings are managed. Some might think of this as the dark side or underbelly of idealization—portraying emotional conflict as aberrant or as a consequence of poor or faulty mentorships. I do not. As I begin to closely examine such conflicts in this section, I want to reiterate what I have stated in the introduction: that is, putting aside cases of mentorship involving individuals with clear psychodynamic pathologies, I do not see emotional conflict as necessarily anomalous nor as a symptom of bad mentoring relationships. Rather, I see the emotional ups and downs in mentorship through a dialectical lens. That is to say, my view—reflecting evidence from interviews with scores of individuals in long-term intense mentoring relationships—is that complicated and conflicted feelings arise in mentorship *because* relationships have grown to be strong and close. Such feelings are, in other words, normal and in many ways signs of the potential for growth.

Under the best of circumstances, idealization entails some measure of surrender. Enthralled, the protégé allows self–other boundaries to become softened so as to internalize the good that the mentor has to offer. As we envision this process, however, one can immediately sense professional and personal vulnerability. The dynamics of possibility that breathe life into idealization can also choke the mentoring process. Aiming to please a seemingly perfect mentor, one's rapture may lead to over-dependency, "good-girl" or "obedient son" syndromes, self-negation, envy, and resentment. (Although not the norm, we also hear of sycophancy, ingratiation, slavish conformity, and other more explicitly dysfunctional dynamics.)

One illustration of this is the protégé who attempts to rework trauma or compensate for lacks in early relationships with parents by relating to the mentor in an overly submissive, compliant, or needy fashion. This way of relating epitomized the early interactions of a mentoring pair of social work professors I spoke with. Somewhat ashamed to tell me this, Petra, squirmed as she admitted that in the first couple of years of her relationship with her mentor, Mitchell, she tended to be "clingy." She said she had had intense feelings for him— nearly spellbound by a man she described as her "godfather." Trying just about anything to gain his approval, she eagerly yet somewhat compulsively offered to run personal errands for him on and even off campus. Opening up to me with considerable psychological percep- tiveness and a palpable desire to work through these issues, Petra said she had been aware for some time that her good girl compliance and intense adoration towards Mitchell had been a pattern starting earlier in her life. She had played it out before, albeit ambivalently, with other teachers and sports coaches in the past—Mitchell was simply the next in line to serve as an unwitting catalyst of her transference-based long- ings. For his part, Mitchell seemed unaware of the back-story of his protégé's psychic drama—sometimes, he said, he had tried to help her "outgrow the neediness" by letting her know she did not have to go so overboard in trying to please him. Other times, he confessed to becoming exasperated and "turned off" by her fawning. Both were worried that Petra lost a good deal of self-esteem in the throes of this dynamic.

It is not hard to imagine how idealization might stir up feelings of inadequacy. Sizing oneself up against a puffed up mentor can lead protégés to feeling weak, inferior, under skilled, and lacking by comparison. Discouraged—mainly on the basis of elaborating a fantasy that to please the mentor one must be as perfect or powerful as said mentor appears to be—the protégé may wind up sabotaging his or her own work efforts or become disabled by anxiety or self-doubt. Feeling this sense of smallness in comparison to his highly accomplished mentor, Tom Grimes wrote:

> [Frank's bestseller novel] eclipsed my [first] novel by such magnitude that I dreaded telling him of its existence. I believed the book's publication might diminish his affection for me, and he'd lose interest in the novel he'd expected me to write. He might even feel betrayed. (2010, p. 67)

Whether feeling overshadowed by or basking in the glow of a mentor, the idea that the protégé *reflects something* or *anything* of the mentor can itself become binding. One protégé, Paulina, described an entrapping dynamic that she and her mentor, Marsha, had engaged in for some years at their publishing company. Stemming from a long history of idealizing her super-competent mentor, Paulina came to feel that she was unseen as a separate person. As her mentor's "right hand," Paulina expressed anguish during our interview as she was coming to terms with the fact that her mentor—and now others in the company—had seen her primarily as an extension of herself, a narcissistic appendage, and not as a distinct person in her own right. Expressing a bit of consternation *and* pleasure, both Paulina and Marsha told me that they had become known in their company, in fact, as "frick and frack." Note that the mentor was *also* implicated in this moniker—risking loss of her own distinctiveness in relation to an idealizing protégé.

* * *

The binding quality of idealization also rouses conflict-laden dependency needs. As a protégé gains a sense of being able to lean on another for growth, he or she risks exposure and shame while opening up to the mentor. Already vulnerable by being subordinate in the authority relation, the idealization process enunciates the protégé's dependency position in the relationship. At its extreme, protégé narratives reflect a "without you I'm nothing" theme. In one case, Phoebe—a mid-level editor at a weekly newspaper—felt exceedingly indebted to her mentor, Murray—inflating the latter's contribution to her career to such a degree that she disavowed the significance of her *own* talents and resources in her development, saying "I don't think I would have a career if it wasn't for Murray."

Envy, resentment, and guilt are also in the fallout from idealization. The idealized mentor seems to, and of course does to some extent, possess something that the protégé covets but does not have. Such inequality—sometimes perceived as inequity—can easily trigger hostility for protégés who raise nagging questions such as: Why does it seem so easy for the mentor to perform the work (*when it is so hard for me*)? Why does he get all the glory and the credit (*when I get little or none for work I have done to help him*)? How come she gets to hobnob with all the important people in the field (*and I am in the background*)? Freud, we should remember, noted the origin of this rivalry in the oedipal scene wherein the child both identifies with and wishes to kill one parent so as to claim the exclusive affection of the other. The competition to have what the mentor has or even to surpass the mentor—a topic we will explore in depth in the chapter on generativity—is likely to stimulate guilt.

*   *   *

Without a doubt, the behavior and emotional needs of a mentor figure importantly in idealization tensions. Dramatic tales of mentors demanding adoration—some even extracting it coercively from disciple-like protégés—are common in published mentoring stories—particularly in stories where the relationship has gone bad. Rendered with exquisite nuance by the biographer Elzbieta Ettinger (1995), philosopher Martin Heidegger's mentorship of Hannah Arendt highlights this dynamic by zeroing in on how powerful a mentor can be in pulling the strings of a protégé's captivation:

> When they met, the thirty-five-year old Heidegger, married and the father of two young sons, was finishing the manuscript of *Being and*

Time (1927), a book that would put him in the ranks of the most prominent philosophers of the twentieth century. From their correspondence it is clear that he fell in love with his young student from their earliest meetings in his classroom. And though his passion subsided as time went on, his need to be her idol did not. Until he met Hannah, Heidegger—strict, rigid, hard-working, the son of devout Catholic peasants—seems to have known little of genuine passion ... He needed her in order to breathe fully and deeply, to enjoy being alive; he needed to have her as a "stimulating force" in his life, as he put it. (p. 3)

Heidegger transferred the cult of worship from the lecture hall to his personal relationship with Arendt ... When they were together, taking a walk or meeting on "their" bench, he talked and she listened. (p. 7)

Heidegger was not an aggressive man, at least not in the conventional sense. But his willingness to put [so much] at risk in his pursuit of Hannah reveals a forceful, self-centered nature and a capacity for ruthlessness and cunning. Despite this, or maybe because of it he was an insecure man in constant need of worship and adulation ... which Hannah provided in abundance. (p. 17)

Depending on a mentor's own idiosyncratic proclivities—stemming from his or her own history and personality—and factoring in very real pressures from work or career, he or she can feel compelled to take advantage of the protégé's adoration. This can take a variety of forms including offloading one's work on to the protégé, soliciting constant praise, adopting the protégé's ideas without offering proper credit, making vague career promises to induce loyalty, etc. Phillip Lopate (1994) warns that professors are especially susceptible to inviting this kind of ego-feeding dependency from their students, suggesting insightfully that there is a fuzzy line (where it ought not be) between eros and emotional conscription in the college setting:

As an experienced teacher, I recognise that there is an inevitable, even desirable element of eros, flirtation, seduction in the learning process. At the same time, I think it should be kept within the bounds of metaphor: I disapprove of sex between students and professors, for all the predictable reasons. I am also made uncomfortable by professors who don't get in bed with their students, but who encourage a dependency, in the guise of offering limitless counseling, or who become so dependent on youth's tender buds to perk up their own desiccated juices, that their annual rejuvenation takes on a vampirish tinge. (p. 106)

One should note that while exploitation of a protégé's idealization can be brazenly self-serving and manipulative—certainly the case when a mentor with a full blown narcissistic personality style extracts adulation and then dumps a follower (Silver & Spilerman, 1990)—this behavior is not necessarily malevolent nor out of the norm. Many find pleasure in the emotional attachment that emanates from protégés' idealization *at the same time* as using it to their professional advantage. Encouraging a protégé's enthrallment, that is, may be motivated by both expressive and instrumental aims. Moreover, organizational and career pressures (e.g., productivity quotas, office politics, under-staffing) can also play a role in how mentors respond to or *use* the idealization—particularly if one is in the position of directly super-vising a protégé. However one might judge such behavior morally, emotional engineering of employee feelings is usually considered to be a perfectly legitimate team building technique in corporate culture particularly if it is believed to advance an organization's agenda or even if it just gives a mentor strategic edge over competitors or colleagues. Referring to the bottom-line ethos in corporate life, I have heard mentors attempt to rationalize such behavior in verbalizing reactions like, "I'd have to be crazy *not* to take advantage of the protégé's crush on me . . . after all, we're running a business here and . . . I'm going to leverage all the support I can get."

Obviously, not all mentors take advantage of protégé idealization. Some see it as burdensome, in fact, and feel put upon by it like Mitchell, the social work professor (discussed earlier) who expressed displeasure with having to deal with the protégé's grandiose expecta-tions. The problem with idealization, related to me by one mentor who experienced it as a form of entrapment is that "you hold people to impossible standards and then hate them when they do not meet the impossible standard. Who needs *that*?" Turning the script around, some worried about being exposed as impostors and were conflicted about revealing *vs.* concealing their flaws.

For some, idealization is met with embarrassment or outright disdain stemming from uneasy feelings they have about authority. One mentor's narrative was striking in this way as he declared his ideological aversion to being cast hierarchically—as if from "on high" in an authority position. He had a tough time accepting that he (or anyone) deserved such veneration. Somewhat paradoxically, his protégé seemed not only to know about this aversion but saw *it* as a type of modesty—giving her even more reason to idealize:

> *Paris*: Probably one of the reasons why Matt is such an attractive person is that he does not know his own power or charisma. If he did, he'd have a big head. And he doesn't. He would be perturbed if he thought he was as powerful over me as he is. He doesn't want that.

Other mentors told me they found the idealization disturbing because it minimized their hard work and continuous effort to achieve and accomplish. This created ambivalence in those who wanted to be appreciated for years of working in the trenches, rising through the ranks, practicing and honing their skills, developing allies and networks, and paying political dues. At the same time, they felt entitled to enjoy the fruits of all of this labor and perseverance—including the fact that they perhaps did not at this point in their careers have to struggle as much anymore at doing the work and managing their professional roles.

After circling around the topic for several minutes, Maggie put her finger on what was so troubling to her about the idealization, decrying that it carried with it a pretense that mentors could rise above the emotional stir of ordinary life. To her, idealization flattened the view of the mentor—omitting the human messiness. Although she admitted to there being moments of feeling gratified by her protégé's view of her as "big and important," on balance, she felt it erased a recognition of her private "real" self—a self that was not a caricature of a mentor, but a real human being with plenty of problems:

> *Maggie*: Sure, I have my public self but I have my inner demons too, you know? I'm not always happy. I can sit in the bottom of my closet and cry for an afternoon, you know? And I think, "Geez, boy are you wrong." (laughs) "You wanna be like me? Boy are *you* wrong."

Despite the fact that mentors claim they are uncomfortable with being idealized, they are clearly drawn in by the eros and pleasure of the powerful dynamic. Often, though, mentors are relatively unaware of the idealization, or they sense its operation but cannot pinpoint when it occurs or how it manifests. As stated earlier, idealization is usually communicated in enactments and attitudes of relatedness—

for example, through an eagerness on the protégé's part to listen, heed advice, comply with direction, etc. But such behaviors are easily interpreted as commonplace signs of cooperativeness, openness to learning, and of having an overall positive outlook. In other words, the mentor understands the sanguine engagement to be a good reflection on the protégé, not necessarily as an emotional response to him or herself.

Defensive reactions

How do protégés handle idealization conflicts? How do they navigate the ambivalence that grows out of idealization? Most of the time, protégés move though stances of idealizing and deidealizing their mentors in relatively predictable and adaptive ways. I will cover this process in the next section. For now, I would like to focus on two prototypical defensive responses—to "give up" or "catch up"—that protégés can have when they are confronted with difficult idealization dynamics. I select these two responses to expand upon because psychoanalytic perspectives have much to offer in analyzing and understanding them.

Protégés who view their mentors as magical are especially prone to conflicts about competition and ambition. If the mentor's ideal qualities are believed to have been divined or somehow effortlessly achieved, the protégé can easily end up feeling inferior: badly equipped, lacking the right stuff—defeated from the starting gate, so to speak. This is logical from the point of view of the unconscious. Although protégés wish to identify with the mentor, this may be difficult because the latter's wondrous qualities can seem unattainable. The mentor appears to be in a different league (e.g., superhuman, "born with a silver spoon"). Rather than offering hope of identifying with someone whose example could be emulated—the idealization can thus have the reverse effect. It can dishearten and give rise to passivity—or what I am calling a "give up response."

There is a good chance that a transferential component and neurotic rewards are in the wings for protégés who assume this position. As noted earlier, reviving the oedipal dilemma, the mentor is perceived as having something that protégés want but believe they cannot have. They may withdraw, regress, or deskill to defend against making contact with competitive feelings, ambitions, resentments, anxieties, and self-doubt—evoked in the mentorship, though rooted in early childhood. Put another way, it may feel emotionally safer for the protégé to give up—in the face of what could seem like overwhelming evidence that the mentor is simply superior in his or her talents—rather than face his or her own unconscious aggressive wishes and impulses towards the mentor. Such a defense lets the protégé off the ambition hook as it provides a plausible justification for the mentor's claim to professional goodies while sustaining a fiction that the protégé is not entitled to or does not have the wherewithal to gain access to these. The net result is that the protégé remains tentative about trying to get what the mentor has or removes him or herself from the endeavor completely.

The give up motif is illustrated poignantly in the mentorship between Marcus and Paige, senior and junior administrators, respectively, at a privately held archival firm. While thus far, I have offered quotes from my interviews and brief narratives about mentors and protégés to illustrate various aspects of idealization, the following fleshes out a fuller account of a pairs' reflections about their relationship, also providing the reader with an expanded picture of how idealization unfolds in the context of occupational demands, specific roles that mentor and protégé play in their organization, and work-related events that shape activity and feelings.

*   *   *

Case vignette: When idealization leads to a give up response in the protégé

Once Marcus promoted Paige to be his deputy, the two proceeded to collaborate on a major project of technology conversion—checking in with each other "up to sixteen times a day." This helped Paige be able to observe Marcus's work habits up close. Yet instead of having this new mode of working together on a project serve as an opportunity for Paige to witness the normal struggles and frustrations her mentor might be having in executing a work project, the exposure reinforced Paige's long held and apparently unshakable view of Marcus as a wizard. Paige only became more impressed by Marcus's technical, conceptual, and managerial gifts as the two spent more time together.

> *Paige:* One of the things that was make or break about the entire project is that Marcus has phenomenal abilities to learn quickly . . .[He] sees the

idea of something and applies the awareness next time it comes—He learns faster than anybody I've ever seen .. . . He just has what seems to me an uncanny ability to prioritize. He really sees what's very important to resolve now and what can wait until down the road . . .

Paige was daunted by Marcus who seemed amazingly efficient at integrating information, making assessments, and plowing through the process of authenticating documents at what appeared to be a super-human pace. He had a razor-sharp organizational mind, could spot and correct errors instantly, and was not distracted by minor textual inconsistencies. Part of her amazement stemmed from the fact that Paige herself tended to be overly obsessional about details and painstakingly reviewed and re-reviewed work to craft it to perfection. In time, watching Marcus's speedy agility became an awesome event for Paige—her mentor seemed other-worldly to her. He did not have to pore over documents with micro-attention and could still deliver the work at an ultra-high standard. For a while, Paige's idealization encouraged her to strive to become like her mentor:

> *Paige*: He has incredible initiative . . . vitality, warmth, and drive . . . and just a prodigiously quick, creative kind of thought process . . . He didn't have to digest it like a cow chews her cud for a half an hour for it to be worth anything. He can think of things in very practical terms. He doesn't get bogged down by detail or lost in abstractions when trying to think about how to proceed . . . Seeing that in action definitely inspired me to try to emulate that or at least hone my own thinking so that the issues that arise in my job—I can bring to bear something like that kind of approach.

The motivating effect of the idealization began to dissipate, unfortunately, as Paige and Marcus confronted a major work crisis. Relieved to have someone he could trust to share the enormous workload, Marcus happily delegated to Paige complete oversight for one phase of the electronic conversion project. For a couple of months, things seemed to be going along just fine. Then, while Paige was out of the office on vacation for a few days, Marcus came to discover that her project was weeks behind schedule—so much so that even with an all-out rescue effort, Marcus worried that *he* might lose his job. He was furious with Paige and confronted her immediately upon her return from the vacation.

Oddly and seemingly out of character, Paige could not really provide Marcus with a sensible explanation as to why she had not stayed on top of the project. She claimed that she took at face value the word of employees she supervised that they were keeping up with their assigned tasks but she never actually checked the work itself. This appalled Marcus. He found it almost unbelievable that Paige would not have instinctively known to check up on the work itself. To make matters worse, Paige was not able to explain this kind of lapse any better when some eight months later—only a few weeks before our interviews—almost exactly the same crisis repeated itself.

Both episodes prompted rounds of meetings between the two and attempts to rectify the situation. Although he dreaded doing it, Marcus took to micromanaging Paige's projects—instituting timetables for completion of smaller tasks and on-going meetings to monitor her progress. Marcus found himself lashing out at Paige as he grew increasingly frustrated by his protégé's forgetfulness, lack of focus, and tendency to turn in incomplete work late. Feeling guilty for getting so angry, Marcus would at other times try to be more sympathetic—try to understand Paige's "challenge." According to accounts from both mentor and protégé, Paige would cower during these exchanges, gnaw at her fingernails, and try to hold on to her self-esteem.

In quite different ways, both Marcus and Paige spent a good deal of time during my interviews with them trying to figure out why Paige was having so much difficulty managing her projects. Verging on exasperation, both were deeply troubled and puzzled by the obvious decline in her functioning on the job. Marcus very much wanted to believe that Paige was capable but that some psychological difficulty was blocking her.

Marcus: I don't believe that these are things she cannot do. I believe there's a reason but I don't know what it is.

Bonnie: Do you think she does?

Marcus: I'm not sure. I think what's ensued is that on her end . . . she's become nervous about *not* pleasing, you know? There may be some of that sort of pleasing a person in authority that, in fact, she's doing things poorly that she used to do very well.

Bonnie: You think the anxiety is tripping her up?

Marcus: Yes . . . but I can't really help her with that other than trying to assure her she's not going to lose her job, and she's not going to lose my friendship or any of that. But also trying to say to her, "If you want, we can look at what are you doing and how are you doing it."

It began to dawn on Marcus that Paige may not have been able to fully appreciate what goes into executive level work because *he* made it look so easy. He felt there was a cost for the admiration he'd received from Paige. Although it took him almost a year to realize it, he understood that Paige's overblown picture of him lead to a series of misimpressions about how he worked and what went into sustaining his accomplishments at the company. Paige wasn't seeing the obstacles that he confronted. They were hidden from view.

Marcus had a good deal of insight, I thought, about how this partial and idealized view of him—a freeze frame image at a point in his career when he was probably at the peak of his professional competence—could trigger a give up response in Paige. The following passage captures the sensitivity of the dilemma he found himself in with respect to Paige's aggrandized image of him. It is worth quoting at length:

> *Marcus*: I was a little uncomfortable [with Paige's admiration]—I'm not terribly good with compliments. I thought she may have been, what can I say?—overblowing it—because she was seeing it from a distance . . . I think she saw me as somebody she wanted to emulate to a certain degree . . . She said this to me—she "marveled at my ability to handle so many things at one time and yet be able to control and organize and keep everything going." . . . I think that maybe what she wasn't seeing was all of the anguish that I go through. I'm a very positive person outwardly and outwardly I show strength. But I mean, it takes a lot of work and a lot of effort—it's not that easy. *I mean it looks easy but it isn't that easy.* And I always felt that she was seeing the surface—and wasn't seeing what's behind that and all that goes into it . . . And I felt that maybe she wasn't recognizing that. I mean, this was not just . . .

> *Bonnie*: Magic?

> *Marcus*: Magic, right. Although it had seemed to be magic. And although certain things—yes, you could sit in a meeting and I could say, "What about this idea?" You know, something popped into my head but of course it's coming from experience. Years of experience. I've been in the business for thirty years, practically. So yeah—just by virtue of experience I'm going to probably be able to come up with more ideas. But then the doing—there's still a lot that's involved. Maybe it looked too simple? I don't know. *Maybe I make it look too simple because you only see the end result.* You don't see all that went behind it.

With evident insight and care, Marcus figured out that his protégé's adulation had not served the relationship or mentoring process well. He saw that by eclipsing the hard work that had gone into developing himself in his career, Paige's idealized image of him intimidated her. And he guessed that the anxiety from that was at the root of her declining work performance.

Marcus's words reveal the double edge sword for mentors in general when they're viewed as magicians: Does the mentor want the work to look like it took a lot of effort? Does he or she want the protégé to know about his or her tricks and shortcuts? Does he or she want to expose the protégé to the messiness behind the polished surface? If a mentor wants the protégé to understand the pains of growth, how does he or she model this when having already passed those trials? These questions touch on concerns about generativity, modes of influence, and the narcissistic investment mentors bring to these processes discussed at length in Chapter Five.

For her own part, Paige was not sure what she believed or felt about her work troubles—ambivalent about whether to accept sole responsibility for them or blame part of them on difficulties with Marcus.

> *Paige*: (She sighs before speaking.) I have thought about it a lot and I've gone back and forth about it. And there are times when I say, "Okay, if I hadn't had 60,000 other things to do, if I'd really taken the time to step back and try to assess what was most important to get done, and what needed to be thought through, and just because it wasn't immediately visible on my plate, you know, it was an issue out there—if I'd really taken that time and applied my intelligence, I could have gotten there." But I go back and forth about the same issues. Sometimes I think, damn it, there was *no* way. And I think on some levels I feel about Marcus in general that his expectations are very high and sometimes unrealistically high of people and how they're going to behave and how they ought to behave. And yet he's so robust—and he's such a realist on some levels.

Grappling with trying to figure out who was to blame for her work difficulties, Paige supposed that she was not cut out for the managerial role—that she lacked the mindset for planning, sorting, managing, focusing. In this sense, she felt that Marcus had misread her skills and abilities. Although she was flattered by the way that Marcus pumped her up by insisting that she could become an ace manager, Paige began to think that this was mostly projection on Marcus's part. She was not at all sure that Marcus really understood her abilities all that well.

* * *

In contrast to throwing in the towel, some protégés react to fantasies of magical mentors by trying to catch up to them—anyway they can, *tout de suite*. Placing emphasis on the perception that what the mentor does looks effortless, the protégé may try to acquire what the mentor has as if the *process of development itself* was magical. As if to say, "what my mentor has is marvelous and with a wave of the wand, I shall have that too," the protégé may in a metaphorical sense try to become an adult without having to grow up. Tapping primitive, pre-symbolic psychological wishes, this occurs through imitation, rather than identification. In Chasseguet-Smirgel's (1985) words:

> It is imitation when the child holds the newspaper *like* his father. It is identification when the child learns to read. Imitation means trying to *be* the envied parent and not necessarily to *become* it. This is the domain of magical achievements (p. 111).

> In the definitions of imitation against identification, there is always the idea of magically being able not to *become* big, but to *be* big immediately, thus bypassing the process of maturation (p. 114).

Adopting the catch up position are protégés who make superficial attempts to gain knowledge, skill, or competency that mentors display—looking for short-cuts and trying to skip steps—as if they believe that no work, adversity, risk, or struggle should be required in development. Marlena, a literary agent, puzzled over Paola's dilettantish attempt to acquire a depth of perspective that took decades of hard work for her to cultivate:

> *Bonnie*: I've been finding it really interesting to talk to mentors who, as part of the process of being put on a pedestal and admired, find that one of the issues that's frustrating is the idea that somehow it's magic . . . that what you do and how you do it comes easy.

> *Marlena*: (very animated) Yes! Yes! Yes! Oh yes, I know exactly what you mean! . . . That's so true. It's sort of like if Paola asks me, "Well, what's the *one* book I can read to understand what it took you twenty years to understand!?" (laughing raucously) and then I think (gasps) "Uh oh!" And then I find out that she's *read* the fucking book! That's when I said, "Well read it again!"

The attempt to bypass the process of training and socialization while still aiming to become a professional is not just a psychological aspiration. Cultural ideals also promote the protégé's flight from the pains of learning. Instead of appreciating that human development is a process over a person's entire life—and a collective one at that—we tend to valorize the idea that a person arrives at the doorstep of adulthood fully formed and self-directed with little need for further mastery or support. The idealized mentor, from the point of view of a protégé who holds this fantasy—thus becomes an object to imitate. The protégé makes only a facile or "magical identification" with him or her. However seductive, the quest for magical relief from all struggle, as Salzberger-Wittenberg and colleagues (1999) point out, ultimately leads to disappointment and retards authentic development.

> Teachers, like others in helping professions . . . easily become objects of infantile hopes; someone who will magically cure pain, take away frustration, helplessness, despair, and instead provide happiness and the fulfillment of all desires. We must expect that a person who holds on to the belief that such wishes should and *can* be met will easily feel disappointed, may soon turn away from us in anger, blame us for being totally unhelpful and seek out someone who appears more likely to fulfill his wishes. What is so dangerous in this attitude, and our tendency to fit with it, is that it is anti-development, for as long as there is a persistent belief that the individual does not have to struggle with some frustration and mental pain he is not likely to discover any latent strengths. Most of us do not attempt to stretch our mental muscles unless we have to (p. 28).

As touched on earlier, the emotional needs and behavior of the mentor play an important role in the construction of idealization fantasies—particularly, and perhaps most importantly for this discussion—by encouraging the myth of his or her magic. This is because structural features of the relation expressed in the mentor's everyday demeanor and activity unwittingly foster such an illusion. The fact is that mentors *do* have more experience and expertise than protégés and usually *have* mastered some aspect of work and life roles, or at least, have greater command of these than protégés do. And they may *appear* to sail through their performance on the job; indeed they *may* actually sail through parts of it. Understandably, mentors express a sense of deep satisfaction in knowing that their efforts have paid off: like the magician who performs feats without offering a hint that there is technique behind the illusion—being perceived as wondrous can be heady stuff. For some, it is taken as a sign that they have mastered their professional chops and can show off to the world an easy proficiency and self-sufficiency; it is payoff for years of learning and practice. Reveling like this is not regarded as hubris but rather an earned sense of pride. Some may even forget the toil that preceded the mastery—repressing memory of the difficulties—recalling only the successes and savoring only the moments of achievement.

The fiction that this seemingly effortless performance creates, however, is that the mentor does not and has not ever had to deal with obstacles—like all other mortals—to hone his or her craft, compete with colleagues, develop a professional identity, etc. For this reason, how competent the mentor appears day to day in carrying out work and life roles—how much doubt, vulnerability, error, etc. he or she shows matters. Exposure to seeing the mentor struggle—or lack of it, as we saw in the in case of Marcus and Paige—can diffuse or feed the myth of the mentor's magic.

I have tried to show in this section that idealization can be damaging to the extent that it coheres around fantasies and feelings that disrupt development. This includes fantasies and feelings that generate faulty or defensive identifications with the mentor—offering the protégé either little hope or distorted notions about what it would take to acquire some of what the mentor has; engendering resistance with respect to diving into the endeavor to learn, master new skills, expand knowledge, and mature professionally and personally; and limiting the protégé's capacity to use the mentor as a model, inspiration, and developmental springboard. The projections entailed create emotional conflict and contort developmental space for the mentors as well.

Recap

Just to summarize before moving on: for the protégé, idealization implies an encounter with his or her own sense of lesser knowledge, maturity, skill, etc., relative to fantasies of a perfect, powerful, and magical mentor. The various types of ambivalent responses outlined above are to that encounter with lack. These include the fact that protégés may feel:

- motivated, hopeful, inspired, and challenged by the idealized mentor to strive, grow, and achieve
- dependent, vulnerable, and exposed to shame—fearing exploitation, infantilization, and humiliation by the idealized mentor
- overshadowed by the glare of the idealized mentor—facing conflicts about loss of self and identity

- embattled by envy, resentment, and guilt—anxious about wishes to usurp what the idealized mentor has
- defeated and inadequate—crushed by the thought that they can never possess the magic that they believe is the mentor's quintessence, and/or
- catapulted *to be* mentor rather than *to become like* him or her, mythically believing that based on the mentor's example, development must be a snap.

To the extent that they are aware of it, mentors also have a range of conflicted reactions to the idealization. The ambivalence felt by mentors has resonance with parental concerns. Mentors may feel:

- seduced by projected images of themselves as wondrous
- a desire to be the object of admiration in order to serve as potent role models
- anxious about or burdened by projections of unrealistic expectations
- nervous about taking advantage of the intense ardor that fuels the process, and/or
- annoyed by the way idealizing fantasies erase who they really are and how hard they work.

I turn next to examine the flip side of idealization in mentorship: deidealization.

The fall

One cannot look into idealization in mentorship without taking up its corollary—deidealization. Opposite sides of the same emotional coin, they are both modes of attachment propelled by the protégé's appraisal of the mentor. Whereas idealization lives through aggrandizing images of the mentor, deidealization takes mentor back down to grounded reality. Exulting fantasies and projections give way to the development of a more realistic assessment of the mentor. The mentor is reduced, that is, to human scale. His or her flaws and limitations become more prominent in the protégé's thinking and emotional stance. Adoration is replaced by reservation, skepticism, disappointment, and sometimes disparagement, denigration, and rejection. Under optimal conditions, deidealization leads to an appreciation of the mentor's humanity, helping the protégé to tolerate imperfection in him or herself, and to come to some acceptance that growth can be challenging and at times painful for everyone.

Deidealization typically unfolds in tandem with the protégé's efforts to separate from the mentor and develop a more autonomous professional identity. Crises also lead to deidealization such as when the mentor engages in behavior that exposes the myth of his or her perfection, magic, or power. Two types of deidealization motifs emerged as prominent among the mentors and protégés in my investigation.

A first type of deidealization stems from the impulse to *differentiate* one's identity and starts in mentorship almost from the start of the relationship alongside of the emergence of idealization. That is, it seems to run as a parallel or counter process. Even when idealization is very strong, the protégé usually does not idealize *everything* about his or her mentor. To express one's separateness and primordial desire and capacity to distinguish oneself and one's agency, the protégé almost always finds some faults in his or her mentor.

Recounting their idealized views, protégés tended to split hairs. That is, there were many instances during my interviews in which protégés qualified their praise of mentors by criticizing some aspect of the very quality they were elevating. Paul, for example, was passionate as he lauded his mentor's wizardry as an editor. In the same breath, however, he added that because Michael made decisions so quickly, he was often blunt and dismissive in his manner of relating to employees—qualities that Paul said he hopes not to emulate. Similarly, another protégé expressed disdain of her mentor's style this way: "I hope to be a kinder, gentler version of [my mentor]." This way of leveraging a deidealizing comment to temper idealization was not unusual. Often protégé complaints have an air of nitpicking as if to suggest that the substance of the criticism matters less than the act of asserting oneself as distinct and able—even under the weight of considerable admiration—to assert agency and retain an independent center of gravity.

A second type of deidealization entails *disillusionment*—a loss of belief in the mentor's greatness and all that such a belief has come to represent to the protégé. While it ultimately leads to a crucial phase of maturation for the protégé, this creates more emotional turmoil for the protégé than differentiation. Because mentors inevitably fail to live up to grandiose expectations, deidealization leads to disappointment and a sense of loss. Protégés face difficult truths that mentors struggle and are as flawed and imperfect as the next person. And as it becomes apparent that the mentor will not serve as a ticket to an existential Easy Street, protégés realize that salvation or return to lost paradise—that is, the fantasy of recapturing one's ego ideal—is not an option. The mentor's fall from grace, in other words, is the protégé's as well.

Disillusionment usually emerges over time in relation to the protégé's process of separating from the mentor. Protégés need mentors less for counsel and approval as they master the work and establish themselves within companies or professional fields, among colleagues, and as they become more secure in their own professional identity and life roles. As protégés gain independence and experience at work and life, aspects of the mentor's alleged greatness become demystified, and idealization weakens.

Separation also occurs, in part, as the protégé comes to be able to make more realistic assessments of her mentor. In the usual sequence, protégés will have opportunities to test their inflated perceptions of mentors against reality as the relationship progresses. For example, as protégés observe mentors in a range of work contexts, they can recalibrate their own views in light of new information. One protégé, Phillis—an up and coming painter in New York—noted the startling difference between her earlier, somewhat exaggerated image of her mentor, Melania, and her current view:

> *Phillis:* It's funny because . . . I thought that Melania was *the* most well connected person in the world . . . Now that I'm working in Chelsea, I realize that there are thousands of people who are way more connected than she is or would ever be. It was an awakening for me to realize that. Even though every time I think she's not that well connected—something will spring up and I'll go "There—she *is* pretty well connected," but maybe not as well connected as I originally thought.

Disillusionment over the mentor's influence (or lack thereof) may also occur as his or her career downshifts. That is, protégés who work with their mentors long enough may see them lose stature in their field. Tom Grimes wrestled with this situation as he came to realize that his mentor was having difficulty getting famous author friends to agree to write book jacket quotes for Tom's latest novel:

One morning in his office, Frank called E. L. Doctorow, who had been sent a galley of the book. When Frank reached for the telephone, he looked at me and said, "I love doing this." Yet after the two of them spoke for thirty seconds, it became clear that Doctorow wouldn't be providing a quote. "I understand," Frank said. Briefly they talked about a trip they'd made together to Russia, years earlier . . . Then he stared at a point in space behind me, the way a stage actor *looks toward but not at an audience*. He shrugged. "Well, he can't do it."

I said, "That's fine," knowing Frank had begun to feel powerless with regard to generating praise for the book. (2010, pp. 129–130)

As this scenario suggests, the protégé will probably encounter situations in which a mentor's actual stature—relative to the profession at large, as well as his or her imperfections, vulnerabilities, and waning prominence—come into focus. This will challenge and transform the protégé's fantasies and convictions about the mentor's ideal qualities.

Relief

As a process marked by separation and autonomous growth, deidealization definitely has a liberatory side. The protégé may delight in the strides he or she has made in beginning to carve out a professional identity and enjoy his or her expanded freedom and capacity to more objectively evaluate his or her mentor, career, organization, field of work, life course, etc. The awareness that the mentor is not perfect may come as a great relief. It helps the protégé relax in the knowledge that he or she is, after all, equal as a human being—and the mentor is not, as it turns out, a member of some higher level species or exclusive club.

Interestingly, an illustration of this latter point came from a mentor, Meena, who experienced her own sense of relief as it became apparent that her protégé's idealization had faded—at least somewhat. Some years earlier, glass ceiling barriers and vicious battles with executives led Meena to resign from the real estate firm in which she and her protégé, Pam, had worked. Ultimately, Meena left real estate altogether. Both of these major changes hit Pam hard. After Meena left, Pam felt lost in the company where she and her mentor had worked side by side for the previous five years. Very discouraged, she did not quite know what to make of or how to think about Meena's exit from the company and eventual divorce from the field. But the two did manage to stay connected. Three years after they stopped working together, Meena described the way that Pam continued to cast hope against disappointment in order to buffer the impact of the blow:

> Meena: Pam's still disappointed . . . last weekend she was like, "Do you know that you could call anybody in the real estate business and they'd take you back in a second? You could do whatever you want." And I was like "You know what, Pam, I appreciate you thinking those wonderful things of me but I know that that's not true. I've been out of the field for too long and no, I couldn't 'walk back into it where I left off.' " She's really disappointed that I'm not still in the business and I'm trying to make her understand that I've had enough of it.

At the same time, there seemed to be a silver lining to Pam's disappointment—as least as far as Meena was concerned—in that it had to some degree forced Pam to see her mentor more clearly—that is, to idealize less, and to thus seek her approval less often:

> Meena: I grew to like Pam a lot more in the last year because I felt she was more at ease with me. She didn't have to worry about everything she said and me judging her . . . She has taken me off that pedestal a little bit and she doesn't act and treat me like I'm something superhuman. She treats me more like a person now.

> Bonnie: Do you think there are some limits to being in a position where you're idealized?

> Meena: Absolutely . . . I've seen it myself with people that I've idealized in my own life. You always tend not to be yourself around them because you're afraid of . . . how they're going to judge you . . . Pam wasn't herself around me a lot of the time. Like she spent a lot of time trying to impress me. And she has some very impressive qualities. But she spent so much time doing that, that I was just like "Oh, please . . . it's not necessary."

Though it may end up easing tensions in the relationship by lifting expectations on the mentor and lessening the protégé's intense need to please—deidealization, as noted before, is likely to generate some degree of conflict and, thus, may be resisted by one or both parties. One cannot get around the fact that—even if only in fantasy—deidealization involves a depreciation of the mentor. The essayist and poet Diana Hume George (1994) struggled with this type of relational shift, articulating the pushes and pulls of this change incisively:

A writer can't afford to feel forever awestruck at her own front door. I couldn't sit at his feet anymore, receiving the communion of our sacred rites, the ones through which he'd passed his knowledge to me. I also couldn't figure out how to stand up next to him . . . A holy ghost kept pushing me back to my knees. That mentor-god groundwork dies hard, originary and primary as it is. (p. 41)

Protégés may feel guilty or contrary for breaking away from their mentors as they become more discriminating in how to regard the mentor's advice, behavior, character, etc. Autonomy of judgment is sometimes experienced as a form of sedition or betrayal. In fantasy, protégés may also worry about damaging mentors by deidealizing them—as if the mental act of cutting the mentor down to size involves destruction of something the other actually possesses. Melanie Klein's writings help to alert us that this can lead to anxieties about retaliation and persecution. Finally, the need to hold on to illusions of the mentor's perfection or magical qualities can become so deeply internalized and ritualized as part of the dynamic bedrock of the relationship that the protégé may find the disillusionment—especially a sudden one—very disorganizing.

Context matters

Context influences idealization–deidealization processes in important ways. The professional and organizational situation, as well as the official role relationship between mentor and protégé, usually determine how much and what kinds of exposure the parties have to each other. Mentors and protégés who interact in face-to-face contact regularly have access to a greater range of information about each other than those whose contact is primarily by phone or electronic communication or occurs less frequently. Observing the mentor interact with colleagues, family, and friends at work or in social settings, and having the chance to observe the mentor handle diverse work demands (e.g., meeting deadlines, responding to organizational crises, giving performances or presentations, carrying out routines, offering supervision) adds dimension to idealizing and deidealizing processes. An atypical case—but one that drives home the point—is of a protégé who wound up renting a room in her mentor's flat. Through this very personal and quotidian contact, the protégé had to come to grips with the stark contradiction between her previous fanciful image of her mentor living "the good life" and the far less flattering reality of her mentor as a woman given to bouts of depression and painful social isolation. Hence, the amount and type of contact thus shapes the content and intensity of idealization fantasies as well as the opportunities for testing those fantasies against reality. Generally speaking, the more mentor and protégé come to know about each other, the less idealization there is.

Idealizing–deidealizing processes also seem to be contoured by the presence of other colleagues on the scene against whom the protégé evaluates his or her own mentor. This includes mentors of friends, potential "available" mentors who are newcomers into the organization or professional field, former mentors, etc. Protégés have a tendency to measure mentors against other would-be mentors as a kind of mental exercise or flirtation. Sometimes this has the effect of affirming the protégé's good fortune (as in "My mentor is better than *his* mentor"). Very often, however, the comparisons end up feeding disillusionment. Appraising one's mentor in light of others who are relatively unknown and can thus easily become new targets for idealization, protégés are drawn to consider the trade-offs in working with their particular mentor as opposed to others.

Institutional change also affects idealization–deidealization processes. Among other post-industrial shifts, for example, technology upgrades are especially significant. Where new electronic and computerized machinery is brought into organizations—sometimes calling for production or system overhauls—mentors and protégés can instantly find themselves in an awkward situation with respect to their authority positions. Mentors will not necessarily know more than their protégés—at least technically. In fact, because protégés are younger and more recently trained, they sometimes have a more cutting edge skill base than their mentors. The leveling or reversal of expertise can destabilize the authority dynamics in mentorship. Or, as illustrated by the example of Mason and Patrick, the reversal can be used to humanize the mentor, and soften the idealization for the good of the relationship. Mason, a program director at a city museum, felt strongly that he did not want his protégé, Patrick, to continue to idolize him as some kind of technical guru so he asked Patrick to collaborate with him on creating the website from scratch. Mason, himself, had no previous experience doing this and felt that if they pursued the learning process together, Patrick would have the chance to see that Mason could be "stupid" too. Ultimately, this was Mason's strategy to play down what to him had become a pretentious sense of hierarchy in the relationship. Adjustments like these that attempt to more closely align perception and reality of what the mentor knows and has to offer the protégé have significant implications for the relationship, its emotional fuel, and its benefits.

Final thoughts

I have posited in this chapter that idealization is a vital relational process in mentorship—its potency lies in the ways the self (protégé) imagines becoming greater, enhanced, more perfect, or powerful through a link to the idealized other (mentor). Understanding the psychoanalytic concept of the ego ideal helps us understand the early roots and power of idealization in mentorship. Projected as the ego ideal—mentors serve as beacons of hope that protégés can attain their own sense of mastery and edge towards their own ideal.

The same idealization that can motivate the protégé to work hard, take risks, accept challenges, and strive productively for the mentor's approval, however, can lead to unrealistic expectations and debilitated work performance. Many factors—reality oriented and transference inspired, interpersonal and professional, situational and contextual—determine in what situations idealization will stimulate excitement and drive a protégé to become like his or her mentor or produce feelings of inferiority or envy—sometimes leading to faulty and problematic identification. Even when idealization, on balance, seems to be motivating, protégés wrestle with insecurities about measuring up to the mentor and anxieties over aggressive and competitive wishes.

But idealization in mentorship is fluid. It is never pure, but ambivalent. Protégés begin deidealizing mentors through processes of differentiation and disillusionment from the start of the relationship. Enthrallment never means complete surrender. Idealization fantasies and myths are tested against reality and aggrandizement tends to fade, giving way to a more variegated image and matured capacity to appreciate the mentor as fallible but human—a crucial life lesson in and of itself.

Mentor ambivalence about protégé idealization is also prominent. Narcissistic gratifications serve to promote the adulation while many mentors resist the projections as burdensome, relationally disruptive, and an interference with protégé development. At the core of mentor resistance, however, is a tenacious ambivalence about their role as authority figures.

We turn next to examine similar themes contained in the emotional undertow of loyalty in mentorship.

CHAPTER FOUR

A sticky subject: loyalty in mentorship

Almost every writer who has taken up the question of what makes mentorships tick mentions the significance of loyalty. Embodied in the pledge to stand by another, loyalty is identified as a cornerstone of the emotional tie in the alliance—which is why it is so surprising that little has been explored on the topic. This chapter fills in the gap by looking closely at the character, dynamics, and expression of loyalty in mentorship. My primary aim is to shed light on how loyalty serves as the emotional glue in such relationships. In doing so, the reader will see that mentorship loyalty is far more ambivalent than research studies and popular articles suggest. Detailed accounts reveal that while loyalty is essential to helping mentors and protégés cultivate and sustain an emotional bond, it also constrains parties in ways that engenders difficult feelings and threatens to undermine relationship benefits. Exploring this paradox is critical to gaining a realistic understanding of both the gratifications and risks of loyalty in mentorship, as well as to calling attention to the need for more social psychological complexity and nuance in the perspectives used to analyze these important developmental relationships.

According to *Webster's Dictionary* (1986), the word *loyal* means that one has "unswerving allegiance: faithful in allegiance to one's lawful sovereign or government; or faithful to a private person to whom fidelity is due; or faithful to a cause, ideal or custom." Loyalty "implies a faithfulness that is steadfast in affection or allegiance in the face of any temptation to renounce, desert, or betray." Focused on constancy in allegiance—at the macro level of institutions and the micro-level of personal relationships—such definitions give us only a hint of the emotionally transactional and layered character of loyalty. While it clearly draws on feelings of love, admiration, trust, and fear, we cannot, for instance, view loyalty as an individual emotion. That is, it cannot be understood as being a property of a person as say, grief or shame can. It does not make sense to say one is loyal to oneself, for example, or that one has a feeling of loyalty in the absence of naming an object towards which that emotion is aimed. Rather, people are loyal to each other and hence it is what might be called a social emotion. Like idealization, loyalty is best understood as a mode of attachment and a relational attitude—a position one develops towards an other—which is both an outgrowth of and part of what constitutes the emotional bond between parties. While idealization expresses the protégé's wish to be like his or her mentor and leads to emulation and a vital sense of hope about attaining ideals, loyalty acts as the sealing agent in the relationship, impelling both parties to want to stick by, aid, and protect each another. It functions to hold the relationship together even when or perhaps more consequentially—especially when—times are tough.

Parallel process

Minutes before finishing my first interview with Polina, it occurred to me that one of the reasons I had felt tension during the two hours we sat around her kitchen table talking was that she may have experienced our conversation as breaching the loyalty she felt towards her mentor, Maura. Even though Polina had been away from her executive associate job at an investment firm since taking maternity leave over a year earlier—she was visibly uncomfortable with some of my questions, particularly ones that probed at her disappointments, grievances, and critical judgments about her mentor and the complicated relationship she had developed with her. Polina fidgeted as we spoke. A number of times during the interview, she seemed to come right up to the line of saying something negative about Maura and then back off—pivoting to talk about a sunnier side of their relationship, silence herself, or explain away some troubling behavior.

I wondered whether Polina felt she was betraying her mentor simply by speaking honestly to me about the relationship. Was I overstepping a boundary by asking her to reveal struggles—to divulge something, for example, which could make her seem ungrateful to her mentor? Did our conversation itself feel like a test of her loyalty? It was true that I had promised not to disclose what Polina had said; as part of my confidentiality agreement with interviewees, I vowed not to share any information told to me by one party to the other. Still, I had a nagging feeling that Polina was scared to say anything negative about her mentor. Maybe she did not want to admit these things to herself.

As a social researcher with a clinical background, I wanted to be sensitive to explore conflicts that Polina (or any others I spoke with) might be having in opening up to me about dissatisfactions or feelings they may have previously felt taboo to talk about. I suspected that interviews like this were unique; it is not every day that someone asks probing questions and listens carefully to minute details about one's close relationships—particularly the often under-the-radar alliances with mentors. As I note earlier in the book, many people are ambivalent to even acknowledge their mentorships let alone explore them in depth. So, while I asked, I also listened intently for what was left unsaid or barely said and I watched body language—reading Polina's reserve as a cue to the muzzling character of her loyalty:

> *Polina*: I enormously respect Maura and feel just eternally grateful to her for giving me the opportunities that she has and I always will. She created a career for me. I was sort of floundering and I was doing things I didn't like. And she saw something in me—maybe I didn't even see in myself. She kind of molded me, nurtured me, and I'm very, very fond of her. Over the years, I've learned to overlook the faults that used to drive me crazy and to realize everyone has character flaws.
>
> *Bonnie*: You couldn't be critical about her to other people?
>
> *Polina*: Never, never. It was very rare—maybe at home if it was to my husband. I would come home and tear my hair out sometimes. Because Maura would push me over the edge or drive me crazy that day . . . But

she knew what she was doing because she got everything out of me that she needed to get that department running . . . When I left, people would call me and say, "Maura doesn't know about this, this, and this." And she didn't, because I took care of everything. She didn't have to know about the nitty gritty operation because I was there. (Polina pauses and then looks anxiously at my tape recorder.) Confessing everything on tape—I'm getting nervous.

Bonnie: Are you uncomfortable?

Polina: Well, yeah. It's funny verbalizing these things I would think but never really talked about . . . There were things that Maura—that I really just could not believe. And stepping back from a situation and looking at it—I'd just be horrified . . . I know things she's done that I—(She rolls her eyes and flashes a look of unease, while stopping herself from saying more.) But you know, that's who she is and I stand by her. Sorry.

In these final comments, Polina gave her strongest indication that I was correct in my reading of her quandary. After tiptoeing around the difficulties she had had with Maura, she ended up rationalizing the bad feelings by saying—"that's who she is" and then, as if caught in a transgressive moment of resignation, she quickly reverted to a state of vigilant loyalty—"and I stand by her." In this moment, Polina dramatized the bond and bind of her loyalty to her mentor. As we ended the conversation, she and I shared a metaphorical wink as she let on that she knew that *I* knew she had given me a sanitized version of their relationship. And she issued a parting apology, seemingly, to punctuate the ambivalence stirred up during our time together.

Although there may be fantasies to the contrary—as the previous chapter on idealization also points out—no one truly expects unconditional love from a mentor. Polina realized she must censor herself; it was not safe to talk candidly about her mentor. There are boundaries she cannot cross without consequence. She can be deserted by her mentor. Her career may suffer as a result of a falling out with her mentor. Even her mentor's apparent loyalty towards her does not mean she gets a free pass and that all behaviors will be tolerated. Although she wrestled with it, Polina understood that she must continue to please her mentor to stay in her good graces. Part of a protégé's emotional work in the relationship is to figure out how to do this. And loyalty often plays a significant role.

Asymmetrical reciprocity

While many believe that mentors offer assistance freely—that is, when it is not part of a formal program—and protégés freely make choices about how they will make use of that assistance, it is misleading to frame mentorship as a "gift relationship." Altruism, that is, is not the only reason mentors mentor. Despite the seemingly voluntary nature of the exchange and the fact that parties rarely form any explicit agreement on its terms, there usually is an assumption of quid pro quo. Mentorship narratives show that over time, the process of coming to see oneself and one's role partner as belonging to and having a stake in the relationship paves the way for the elaboration and imposition of expectations and obligations—conscious and not so conscious ones. It is within this nexus of give and take that loyalty finds its home. Concerned with interactional nuts and bolts, mentorship loyalty revolves around the question of "who does what for whom." Royce (1908) was astute on this point in *The Philosophy of Loyalty* when he wrote,

> [The loyal person's] devotion is practical . . . He does something. This something serves his cause. Loyalty is never mere emotion. Adoration and affection may go with loyalty, but can never alone constitute loyalty. (p. 18)

Loyalty, thus enacted, is woven into a system of mutual obligations between mentors and protégés. It is tacitly understood as both an expression of care and an imposition of debt. The gist of a prototypical comment one would hear from a protégé is "If I pledge my loyalty to my mentor, can I count on having his support . . . in offering me the best assignments *or* . . . when it's time to recommend me for a promotion?" And although mentors are less likely to verbalize expectations, some version of the following sentiment is almost always implicit as in "If I remain loyal to my protégé by sparing her from company lay-offs . . . *or* . . . by showcasing her work to colleagues, can I expect her to pitch in to carry out some of my tedious labor intensive time-consuming tasks . . . *or* . . . Can I expect him to carry on my traditions, my values, my ways of doing business?" The anticipation of reciprocity that lays the foundation of loyalty is captured well by legal scholar George Fletcher when he writes that "loyalty gets its grip in relationships with others"

(1993, p. 14). The elusive but ineluctable dualism of loyalty as both a bond and a bind crystallizes in the image of it as something that *grips*.

Sometimes starkly, but most often with varying degrees of nuance, mentors and protégés articulate the feeling that they owe each other and are entitled to make claims on each other for such things as time, favors, plum work assignments, free labor, endorsements, sympathy, ego boosting, contacts, a listening ear, the inside scoop, emotional succor, etc. Themes of sacrifice, protection, pardon, rescue, advocacy, gratitude, cocooning, and devotion are embedded in stories about what mentors and protégés do for and expect of their other half in the name of loyalty.

Margot, a fifty-something year old mentor in a high-tech start-up firm did not mince words as she offered a rather unsentimental view of mentorship as based on a "I'll scratch your back if you'll scratch mine" mentality:

> *Margot*: One of the things I learned from my own mentor fifteen years ago was that nobody just nurtures you. They want something in return. There's got to be reciprocity. People nurture you because they want to also be promoted and they want to look good and have a team that's a star team. If you're going to do that for them, it's going to make them look good. The more responsibility they get, the more you can have. There has to be a mutual need. There is no human being on earth that just gives and expects nothing in return. You have to be almost a saint to say, "I'm going to do this and I'm going to keep on just doing it and doing it . . ." and all you get back is the pride of knowing you did it? It doesn't work . . . There has to be something reciprocal.

Protégés are well aware of this give back dynamic. Patricia muses that, in fact, this may be what makes mentoring different from parenting or, at least, different from the fantasy image of selfless parenting:

> *Patricia*: It's a two-way street . . . absolutely . . . I don't believe that mentoring is a one-way street. I wouldn't think anyone would feel that way. I don't think you can get involved in a mentoring situation if you aren't getting something back from the person who is the protégé because why would you mentor someone that you didn't—wasn't—unless you're really trying to be a parental figure (chuckles), I would guess.

Pete learned that reciprocity in the form of loyalty seems to be contingent on utility; when he is useful to his mentor—in ways that can advance their firm's financial services business ventures—he is kept close, otherwise he falls out of his mentor's orbit:

> *Pete:* Michael approaches situations very strategically and always with an eye to what his interest is in them. And so, there are occasions when you're useful to him—your relationship is very close . . . When you're not, he can be very distant and, you know, sort of icy. There's a certain amount of sidling up and then pushing away that goes on.

For better and worse, there *is* some way that the protégé is expected to show appreciation and give back. Loyalty—in its many forms of expression—conveys this gratuity. In fact, for protégés, loyalty is indispensable as a currency of exchange. At the same time, because mentorship is an authority relationship, the dynamics and expression of loyalty are inherently asymmetrical. Obviously, reciprocity in mentorship does not mean equality or sameness of exchange. By definition, mentor and protégé are not equally beholden to each other; the protégé owes the mentor more and in a different way than the mentor owes the protégé. Exercising influence on behalf of one's protégé is the standard way for mentor to express loyalty. Because of his or her position and experience, the mentor has the resources, capacity, and responsibility to look after and thus demonstrate loyalty to a protégé in ways that the protégé cannot reciprocate. Loyalty as enacted in various forms of material and emotional labor is one type of offering the protégé *can* make in return for the mentor's special attention and assistance. (Note that I use the term "offering" here—marking the ritualistic quality of how loyalty is expressed—a feature to be more fully elucidated later in the chapter.)

For Pierre, showing loyalty is both the avenue to and payback for getting the best exposure for his articles in the daily newspaper:

> *Pierre:* The reason that I'm loyal to Merri is because she's extremely good at getting stories placed and getting reporters good visibility in the paper. There's an enormous variation among the editors as to their talent in doing that . . . I mean, the worst thing that can happen is that the story sits on a budget for a week . . . and the story doesn't run. It doesn't matter if anybody's read it or if there's a good or bad reason—it just gets stale. And so, if you've got an editor who knows when to promote a story, how to get good display of it, you want to stick by them.

Returning the favor of being given so many career breaks, Pamela, now a seasoned editor in a pharmaceutical publishing firm, shows loyalty by shielding her mentor from embarrassment:

> *Pamela*: It's a love-hate relationship. I'd say this one is more love than hate. But there were times where I really was angry with her over things that she would make me do at the office to quote, "save face." Yet she would go out of her way to make sure that I had every opportunity possible that the company could offer me . . . Other people who started at the same time I did and did not have managers who cared as much as Marta, stagnated, or left, or got nothing. Marta made sure that every opportunity was made available to me.

Though, on balance, the positive outweighs the negative for Pamela, this passage underscores loyalty's paradox. On one hand, Pamela feels pressure to stand by her mentor and to do what is expected and necessary to help protect her mentor's reputation. Her mentor has opened doors for her that might have otherwise stayed closed. Beyond feeling a profound sense of debt, Pamela loves this woman. The two have become emotionally close over the years sharing in work pursuits and friendship. At the same time, Pamela recalls times of having been furious at Marta because she felt almost forced to do things to cover for her and in so doing, she felt she compromised her own integrity and good standing at their company. In this way, Pamela's example shows how one can be held by both the emotionally rich connection and sometimes crippling obligation that tend to coalesce in mentorship loyalty.

Exclusivity by exclusion

Part of what gives loyalty its holding power is that it articulates a boundary around the pair. It signals commitment and declares that the parties feel a sense of "we-ness" as dyadic attention and affection become more pronounced. This is because loyalty flirts with exclusivity as mentor and protégé share something special that leaves or pushes others out.

In fact, in order to create this "community of two," loyalty requires a third term. That is, developing the sense of we-ness depends on the existence of outsiders—those who are de facto excluded from the "we." "Stand by me" would be a meaningless phrase unless it contained the implicit understanding that one will not abandon the other in order to side with someone or something else. Thus, loyalty entails sacrifice and restraint. When loyalty is tested, someone or something—for example, a principle, a person, a part of the self, or a belief—will have to be rejected to prove one's loyalty towards the other. Indeed, the fullness of loyalty, it could be argued, can be measured by the extent to which temptations to betray are resisted. "If I pledge my loyalty to you this means I will vouch for you, protect you, hold your confidences, and cover for you during difficult or controversial moments. I won't walk away from you during crisis, undermine your efforts, nor spoil your reputation. My good will towards you can be trusted." Note that in all of these promises, loyalty is conveyed by vowing not to desert the other or take up an opposing principle. The point again to underscore is that the pair defines itself *as a pair* against or in light of something outside of itself. As we will see, this is critical because, of course, mentors and protégés do not operate in a vacuum but rather interact with a world of colleagues and organizational actors—any of whom can play the role of the "third term" in enunciating or threatening the pair's loyalty.

As one might guess, this motif—that of dyadic loyalty forged in the context of a third party—contains elements that can set off all kinds of oedipal maneuverings in mentoring relationships. We will see later in the chapter a case vignette illustrating how mentors and protégés conscript and "use" others from their professions and companies to mark relational boundaries and solidify the allegiance between the pair. For the moment, suffice it to say that residues of oedipal strivings show up as protégés compete with others for mentor's special attention or when they try to reap something in the organizational or professional bounty that might have once seemed available only to mentor (e.g., recognition, staffing resources, company perks). Classic stories of famous mentoring pairs depict emotional quandaries as protégés approach the point of surpassing their mentors. Central to the conflict in such scenarios are feelings of betrayal—wrenching for the pair and not infrequently, the precursor to the relationship's demise.

Beyond the somewhat predictable dynamics of competition and the strains this places on dyadic loyalty, other oedipal themes are activated by mentor–protégé exclusivity. Resonant of a time when a child becomes conscious of the world apart from the mother–baby dyad—a world that requires the kindling of ambition, independent navigation of alliances, delay of gratification, and civilizing of one's impulses and behavior—protégés come to realize that they can and indeed, want to separate, relying on the mentor for some things but not everything. As the protégé becomes increasingly aware of the mentor's limitations, he or she is also being energized by the license to assert agency—that is, to do for one's self and to reach out to new people in the organization or profession for counsel and connection. Thus protégés are challenged to stay attached to mentors while coming into their own. Oedipally charged loyalty in this context is political. As Hirschman's seminal "loyalty, voice, exit" thesis (1970) helps us to understand, the protégé figures out that staying put—that is, remaining loyal instead of turning to exit the relationship—is a way to try to work things out, using voice to get some of what one wants, that is, even if it is not everything.

An example, here, will be useful. Long believing that her mentor, Michael, and his business partner, Carl, got on well, Paris discovered that there was a growing rift between the two men. To her dismay she figured out that she, in fact, was in the middle of it. Co-owners at a San Francisco gallery that helped launch her career as a painter, Paris wrestled with the trappings of her loyalty towards Michael:

> *Paris*: I never in my wildest dreams thought I'd be in this position. Michael is so wonderful, championing my work, helping me along in this really difficult choice to make art my life. When he asked me to bring transparencies to show him my latest work, I didn't have any idea that it was because he didn't want to ruffle feathers with Carl. He didn't want Carl to see me bring in my actual sketches—even though I had done that so many times before—you know, to get Michael's critique. Now I understand of course . . .
>
> Michael wanted the fact that he was treating my work in a special way to be just between us. Carl didn't want him to do me any favors; other artists that Carl was sponsoring were amazing but they weren't getting to show work like I was . . . funny thing is that while Michael was trying to make it seem like he was playing things down between us so Carl wouldn't be put off, I was wondering what it might be like to get to know Carl better. He was definitely less impetuous than Michael—and certainly since the gallery was originally part of Carl's family, I did think that maybe I shouldn't alienate him. I love Michael and I owe him so much. I don't want to be in the middle of their feud. I'm trying to figure out how to talk to Michael about this. But I feel so guilty about it all.

Needless to say, dyadic allegiance among mentors and protégés in a professional or organizational context can be a precarious affair. As alluded to in the above example, loyalty breeds favoritism; by gearing his or her loyalty towards a special employee or colleague, the mentor engages in preferential treatment. As Fletcher (1993) points out, this is inevitable because even in a world that holds moral impartiality as a virtue, the ideal of equality cannot be achieved. Loyalty lives in the world of personal attachments to particular others, while impartiality exists in the realm of abstract universals. Such a bias can have a significant impact on parties in the mentorship and their interactions with others. So while there is a good deal of evidence to suggest that creating and sustaining a tight and even exclusive working relationship can be tremendously productive and satisfying, it can easily set off inter-colleague hostility, jealousy, and organizational mistrust.

Notwithstanding such perils, it is not unusual to hear about mentors and protégés who close ranks—directing most of their loyalty toward each other rather than to their companies. Taking the risk to turn allegiance towards one another rather than out to the organization can make sense for individuals whose organizations and jobs seem insecure. Priya, a mid-level manager at a municipal hospital about to be folded into a larger conglomerate company, ruefully acknowledged that loyalty between mentors and protégés can supplant loyalty to the organization.

Bonnie: How do you figure what makes you so loyal?

Priya: Well for one thing—I love Marlin. I mean he's very close to me and he's my boss. I respect him. My loyalty is to him rather than to an organization because an organization—doesn't have feelings. I've seen them fire—I don't place any faith in the organization as a whole. I place it in certain key people who have either gained my respect or that I feel are fair or who genuinely care about the people that work in a company rather than profits.

Howell Baum, an urban planner and organizational analyst points out that in the way that Priya suggests, mentorship is intrinsically seditious (1992). Organizational drift can propel this trend toward mentorship loyalty with obvious cost. A mentor–protégé pair may cut themselves off from colleagues, professional leaders, or the company or field as a whole.

Emotion, calculation, duty

While deep-seated feelings provide fuel for loyalty in mentorship and psychoanalysis certainly sheds light on the childhood rooting of such feelings, evidence from my talks with mentors and protégés suggest that there is more to the story. There are other pulls to be loyal in this type of relationship. In part, this is because mentorship falls between the lines of professional and personal relationships. It is a liminal relationship—not exactly a friendship, plainly not a parent–child connection, not a teacher–student relationship in any traditional sense, and not merely a boss–employee alliance. Still, because it resembles and, in some cases, builds upon each of these types of relationships, it taps the motivational logics that undergird them. Borrowing from Flam's (1993) scheme of "multiple selves" that proposes that individuals are made up of three selves—the emotional, the normative, and the strategic—one can identify three strands of motivation that give rise to loyalty in mentorship (see Figure 4.1). Mentors and protégés develop a sense that they want to or should stand by each other and act upon this based on a mix of emotional motivations, value and normative considerations, and rational, self-interested, instrumental calculations. These motivations—some conscious and some not—are intertwined and impact each other. I am separating them here only for heuristic purposes.

Emotion-based loyalty can be either positively or negatively oriented. On the positive side are emotions such as gratitude, love, idealization, desire for connection, respect, trust, and protectiveness—leading to voluntary loyalty. A person develops loyalty because he or she wishes to; the offer to stand by mentor or protégé is based on a basic good feeling about the role partner and belief that loyalty will enhance the satisfaction and rewards of the relationship. There is nothing exacted or coerced about this kind of loyalty. On the negative side are emotions that give rise to compulsive loyalty such as fear, anxiety, and guilt. One experiences loyalty as a "must" out of fear, for example, of the material or symbolic consequences of disloyalty. The fears that compel one to be loyal can, of course, be reality-based (e.g., threats of job or income loss) and/or fantasy-inspired (e.g., imagined loss of esteem for minor transgressions). Compulsive loyalty—suggestive of the replay of earlier psychic conflicts—may also be driven by neurotic over-investment in the other person. This is illustrated by the

LOYALTY MOTIVATIONS IN MENTORSHIP			
Emotional		Strategic	Normative
Positively-oriented	Negatively-oriented		
Loyalty which arises out of emotional dynamics associated with:	Loyalty which arises out of emotional dynamics associated with:	Loyalty which arises out of rational calculations regarding:	Loyalty which arises out of conformity to moral and societal codes regarding:
– gratitude – love – idealization – respect – trust – protectiveness – generative urge	– masochism – fear of loss – guilt – denial – coercion – excessive narcissism – excessive dependency	– professional and career aims – political concerns – labor needs – organizational goals	– the socially expected, proper, and "right" stance or attitude to assume toward another

Figure 4.1

protégé who becomes masochistically slavish or fervently allied with a mentor even in the face of mistreatment or rejection. It is also seen in the mentor who feels driven to stick with a protégé who cannot seem to do the job. I call this type of emotion-based loyalty negative because it is enacted as a kind of false compliance. One invokes loyalty to protect the self from internal and external pressures and threats, not because the loyalty expresses a genuine or freely tendered commitment to the other.

Loyalty is also generated by strategic considerations. Strategic issues that lead to loyalty link to instrumental goals aimed at maximizing self-interest and minimizing cost. The strategic calculation to be loyal is a conscious activity, and its expression comes in the form of surface acting and emotion management. That is, it involves emotional work based on rational assessment of choices reflecting professional and career goals, political concerns, and organizational ambitions rather than emotional needs, wishes, fantasies, and anxieties. It comes from the part of the self that is motivated by beliefs about how a person must appear in the situation to make the right impression; that is, the impression that is most likely to yield the desired response. This perspective on the strategic shaping and display of emotion referred to by sociologists as "emotional labor" (Hochschild, 1983) helps us understand the more consciously manipulative and self-serving side to mentor–protégé loyalty.

Finally, loyalty is motivated by normative and moral concerns. One is loyal because it is the expected and socially proper response. The work by Callahan and McCollum (2002) importantly advances the idea that emotional expression is regulated not only by the actor's internal state but also by a web of social rules. For instance, loyalty is considered an appropriate attitude to show deference towards authority figures. It is not necessarily linked to positive feelings—for example, one can strongly dislike a military sergeant or subordinate and still vow not to betray them. Nor is it linked to utility—one who makes a principled decision to be loyal to someone else is not looking to maximize self-interest. The underlying standard for normative loyalty links to ideals about duty, morality, and conformity. One could think of this as the superego layer of loyalty. It is the aspect of loyalty guided by conscience—as the right and proper stance.

It is worth reiterating that none of these types of motivation operate without influence from the other. Loyalty is often based upon a blend of these motivations even though they can be contradictory. Clearly, in the context of complex commitments, the *right thing to do* is not always the same as the *strategic thing to do,* nor are these always in sync with what one *feels inclined to do.* Such pulls and pushes give rise to dilemmas that mentors and protégés try to reconcile. Mark, a forty-eight-year-old HR director, for example, reflected on the kinds of internal debate he regularly has with himself when he considers how far he should go to demonstrate his loyalty towards his protégé, a fellow he had hired into the assistant director position almost five years earlier:

> *Mark:* Should I have stuck my neck out for Paul because he covered for *me* when I missed a critical meeting with a new client? I figured if I did, I might catch hell from this one colleague who seems to have radar out on me. She always tries to shut me down or make me look Pollyanna-ish when I try to help Paul. She makes it seem like Paul can't do for himself. But I felt I owed him . . . he really counts on me.

By examining emotional, strategic, and normative motivations, one can see where the ambiguities of loyalty arise and how these are experienced and worked through by mentors and protégés. Typically, loyalty rides a fine line between enrichment and constraint. The following impressions of a thirty-five-year-old protégé who rapidly ascended to management from an entry-level position at a data analytics firm, incisively show that emotional tensions can arise when all three strands of loyalty motivation are at play.

> *Patricia:* I don't know that Meryl ever really wanted me to see her on a pedestal—I don't think that was her intention. I think she wanted me to respect her and that's where loyalty comes in. I think she needed that . . . She felt she could get that from me. And she did. It's sort of the foundation of our relationship.
>
> *Bonnie:* You keep emphasizing your loyalty.
>
> *Patricia:* Yes, I know. Loyalty is an odd word. Like when someone tells you something in confidence, I respect that. If Meryl would come to me in confidence, I totally respected that and demand that from others around me. I felt a sense of obligation—I owed Meryl because she gave me this break. You don't turn your back on that. You have—I don't know— a code of honor. I sound like I'm in the Mafia or something! It worked for both of us I think.
>
> *Bonnie:* And you couldn't be critical about her?

Patricia: Never at work. To subordinates, certainly not. And colleagues— occasionally a peer that had worked there for a good chunk of time and was also a direct report to Meryl—she and I would commiserate once in a while—like, "Can you believe what she said in that meeting today?" kind of thing. But never beyond that. We never conspired to do anything. The other woman wanted to but I couldn't bring myself to do anything.

Bonnie: Why? Is it because it would make you feel too guilty . . .

Patricia: Guilt's a good thing, yeah. I was also worried about my own career. Meryl's pretty powerful and manipulative and she knows how to push people's buttons. And I definitely saw her in action. She could really get people do to what she wanted. And I certainly didn't want to be on her bad side for that reason. She's very powerful that way.

Patricia's account splices together a range of reasons to be loyal in mentorship. She believed she owed the loyalty based on a mixture of heartfelt appreciation and respect on the one hand, and as a matter of principle (e.g., "a code of honor") on the other hand. She also sensed that her mentor expected the fidelity. And she was right at that. During our separate interview, Meryl, the mentor, was forthright about this expectation. At the same time, Patricia was afraid her mentor would retaliate or make her life difficult if she were to behave in a disloyal manner—spoke badly of her, conspired to undermine her reputation in anyway—calculating that it was in her best interest career-wise to maintain her allegiance, despite the lure of opportunities to stray or betray. The loyalty dilemma for Patricia came from the tension between the obligation and strategic good sense to remain loyal, and the emotional pulls to break away and voice dissent. Similar to most mentors and protégés I have met, Patricia found she had to negotiate with herself as to what role duty, instrumentalism, and "following or swallowing feelings" as she put it, would play in figuring out whether and in what fashion to stand by her mentor. Although these motives were occasionally aligned, it was usually the case that something had to be given up or compromised. Indeed, as will be discussed in the next section, it is through the display of sacrifice as well as other forms of renunciation and self-negation, that loyalty is usually dramatized.

Ritualized enactment

Expressing loyalty in mentorship often takes the form of enactments or *rituals*. Sennett (1980) characterized ritual as "an emotional unity achieved through drama." This is a fitting description of what goes on as mentors and protégés act out the terms of allegiance towards each other. As noted earlier, loyalty must be performed—it involves work; there must be tangible proof of it. Still, many gestures and interactions are symbolic—the emotional meanings and effects of the actions go beyond whatever purpose can be gleaned from the surface behavior. The actions are meant to be interpreted as signs of care, reliability, protectiveness, and as confirmations of commitment to the relationship. We commonly think of loyalty in almost melodramatic terms as in "sticking one's neck out," "going to the mat," "going above and beyond," "going out of one's way," and of course, the ultimate, "laying down one's life for the other."

Fletcher (1993) makes a useful distinction between minimum and maximum loyalty by highlighting the role of ritual. While minimum loyalty is satisfied by the condition of non-betrayal, maximum loyalty requires more than the avoidance of betrayal. According to Fletcher, the latter taps into a profoundly emotional dimension—expressed in rituals of attachment and devotion. The mentor evidencing minimum loyalty, for example, might not speak disparagingly of a protégé during a company controversy, but also might not risk his or her own reputation to actively protect the protégé. Maximum loyalty, on the other hand, entails going beyond the call of duty—such as when a mentor vigorously defends the protégé or offers the protégé opportunities to work on high visibility assignments that—whatever the outcome—will reflect back and affect his or her standing in the company or profession. The devotional dimension of loyalty is expressed through rituals involving personal risk, sacrifice, and staking out boundaries around the mentorship alliance (e.g., by "taking sides").

Numerous examples from conversations with mentors and protégés richly illustrate the way devotional or maximum loyalty is acted out through ritual. One protégé, for example, emphasized the fact that her mentor came to her rescue when administrators threatened to move her into a windowless office:

Percy: At one point when they were rearranging the unit, they were going to put me in a cubicle—something that would have enraged me to the point where I might have quit . . . And [my mentor] *absolutely refused to let them do that.*

Another protégé appreciated the fact that her mentor insisted that she be invited to important meetings with company executives. This signaled the mentor's avid commitment to her:

Pietra: She wouldn't just take me to meetings with upper management, but she would make sure *they* invited me. She would say, "Make sure Pietra is invited to that." She always let people know that she valued me enough that I should be in the meeting to hear the information first-hand—that I may have some important input.

Helping to position the protégé in just the right spot in a company or professional context characterized a range of efforts described by mentors. In some cases, the goal was to engineer positive working relationships between protégés and other key figures in the organization, in other cases mentors wanted to do the opposite—that is, to distance protégés from collegial crossfire, and yet in still other cases, the effort was to showcase a protégé to otherwise inaccessible executives. High drama loyalty enactments during turbulent organizational periods were recounted by several mentors who fought to spare protégés from layoffs. In an especially tension-filled case, one mentor literally had to choose between her protégé and another longtime colleague and friend when her agency downsized.

Before she resigned, Melinda went the extra mile to write a letter for her protégé, Pasha, to remain in the company file after her own departure. In this way, the mentor hoped to extend her efforts to campaign for this protégé for years to come:

Pasha: Melinda wrote me a review before she left Darlington—before she gave notice that she was going to be leaving. She wanted to make sure that it was on my record. She wrote me this incredible review.

Another trend was for mentors to shield protégés from trouble when work suffered or when colleague relations got strained—even if it was the protégé's fault. This was based on a belief that *they* should take the flack for work-related crises and insulate protégés from job jeopardy.

Mitchell: I will never pass the buck. You don't blame people who work for you because *you're* supposed to be monitoring their performance. And if you're not, then you're not doing your job. I never would lay Parth out to dry.

Each of the above examples contains devotional and ritualistic elements of loyalty. One party—in all cases described thus far, the mentor—risks or sacrifices something or extends him or herself to protect, endorse, or gain access to opportunities for the other. At the same time, the arguably routine activities contained in the examples suggest that to demonstrate loyalty, mentors need only carry out mentoring functions (e.g., protect, teach, advocate, sponsor). And presumably they have the personal, professional, and organizational resources with which to do so (e.g., clout, talent, skill, networks). Nevertheless—and here is the most critical point—while the mechanics of loyalty may be embedded in the mentor's usual repertoire of career-enhancing functions as part of the mentoring job so to speak, narratives depict these activities as having a dramatic quality. That is, they are not carried out in a perfunctory manner. Descriptions of mentor interventions are ardent, conveying recognition of commitment to stand by the protégé. The mentor's steadfast and at times zealous willingness to share these resources, in other words—in the name of looking out for the protégé's welfare—affirms that the protégé and mentorship are extra-special. The expression of loyalty elevates the importance of the protégé as it forges expectations of solidarity and reciprocity.

Therein lies the rub. As loyalty enactments strengthen and enhance mentorship commitments, they also give way to emotional binds. The good feelings of communion contain the seeds of obligation for sacrifice and other types of duress. For example, while Percy was grateful to her mentor for insisting she get an office with a window among other perks, she also eventually got a promotion that triggered guilt about surpassing her mentor in the firm hierarchy. While the mentor orchestrated good exposure opportunities for Pietra at meetings with company executives, Pietra felt obligated to take the fall for decisions her mentor made that adversely affected other employees. While Melinda's "glowing" letter for Pasha helped to sustain a bond that outlived her tenure at their workplace, it aroused suspicion in the company president about the mentor's invisible, yet seemingly ongoing influence over this protégé. While Mitchell took the upstanding position to cover for his protégé's mistakes, he suffered personally and took a professional gamble by staying committed to Parth in the face of the latter's debilitating work performance.

Mentors clearly feel torn between wanting to do well by and honor understandings they establish with protégés, but are anxious about making choices that might be perceived as a breach. They realize it is risky to remain loyal particularly in instances when they fight for protégés whose professional inadequacies are apparent to colleagues, as well as situations in which they entrust protégés with secrets or other types of potentially embarrassing or confidential information. Still, as the examples above suggest, the sense of being caught between the bond and bind of loyalty tends to be a good deal more intense and impactful for protégés than it is for mentors because of the sense of debt embedded in their one-down position. For one thing, how the protégé can show loyalty is not so clearly scripted. By definition, protégés are not in a position to repay or engage in equal exchange with mentors as noted earlier; they lack the professional capital to do so. Hence, they have little alternative but to demonstrate loyalty symbolically. And they do so in ritualistic enactments of material and emotional labor that seem to conveniently convey allegiance, deference, and gratitude in one fell swoop.

> *Melissa:* [My protégé] came over the other day and I had to empty the garbage and I said, "Patsy, I've just been noticing how much you must have emptied the garbage in the last year and a half because I can hardly remember emptying the garbage the whole time you worked here and the garbage fills up so unbelievably quickly in this office! I just can't even believe it." She looked at me smiling and rolled her eyes . . . It was like an acknowledgement of the fact that she had done really boring shit work without a peep—without a peep! She never complained. And so, there's that kind of acknowledgment that I can be just so obsessed and so out of it. She knows that that's how I am . . .

The protégé who assiduously joins in with the mentor's work projects becomes loyal to the mentor as they devote themselves to their work or cause. As the task becomes redefined as "our work," the boundary around the pair and ensuing dyadic allegiance is emphasized. Long stretches of time in the relationship can revolve around cycles of joint work. Protégés frequently reminisce about especially grueling phases of work as if making it through these times—toiling hard and going the extra mile for the mentor—earned them a badge of honor. With few exceptions, mentors I spoke with routinely depended upon protégés to perform a range of work duties—some menial, some detail-oriented, some intelligence-focused, and some operational and carrying a high level of responsibility. A sampling of these diverse forms of labor by protégés includes: walking dogs and doing domestic errands to free up the mentor to devote time to artistic endeavors, volunteering for work assignments that entail travel to enable mentor to stay home to care for children, "spying" on colleagues to bring back sensitive information to the mentor, and sharing in the "thinking demands" with a mentor to plan and carry out a technological overhaul in a company's production system.

Later in a mentorship, as protégés come into their own, they may have accrued their own professional capital that can be used to repay the mentor's loyalty in more substantial ways—for example, by publicly acknowledging mentors in memoirs and testimonials, connecting mentors to expanded networks of colleagues, and promoting the mentor's work to the world outside of the organization. According to Ettinger (1995), for example, one could say that by the 1950s—when Hannah Arendt and Martin Heidegger reunited after a long hiatus—Arendt more than compensated her mentor by serving as his "goodwill ambassador" in the U.S., defending him against what for a time she believed were unfounded charges of his anti-Semitism. "The prestige she enjoyed in the American intellectual community, of which Heidegger certainly was aware, was a precious asset" (p. 6).

> After the 1950 visit, Arendt—who had only one year earlier vehemently opposed the publication of Heidegger's work—became his devoted if unpaid agent in the United States, finding publishers, negotiating contracts, and selecting the best translators. Above all, she did what she could to whitewash his Nazi past . . . For Heidegger it was natural to regard her labors as a privilege he accorded her, for in so doing he proved that he trusted her. (pp. 78–79)

It needs to be stressed that similar to the case of the mentor's demonstration of loyalty, protégé loyalty emanates not only from the performance of the work task but from the *intention* that one brings to the work activity. The loyal protégé approaches the work, in part, with a sense of mission and a loftier goal. He or she does the work *for* the mentor, for the advancement of *their* projects, and for his or her own good standing with the mentor. Contained within the protégé's enthusiasm to serve is a piece of emotion management; the *esprit de corps* conveys a feeling tone of alliance and allegiance. One mentor remembered a zestful protégé saying, " 'I will do the best job in the whole world for you'—that's exactly how she put it and I knew she would. I could just feel it."

Emotion work

Beyond displaying enthusiasm in carrying out work tasks, protégés engage in other forms of emotion work to act out loyalty as they perform various caretaker roles and manage delicate situations for mentors. As a *gatekeeper*, for example, protégés screen contacts to liberate mentors from unnecessary details and distractions. Sometimes protégés act as *emissaries* when mentors have reputations of being difficult to deal with. In this latter role, protégés try to protect mentors if they think others in the organization see *them* as the more amiable and accessible partner in the duo. Conversely, when called for, sometimes protégés accede to play the role of *scapegoat*. One protégé, for example, who tacitly agreed to play "the heavy" did so partly to preserve an idealized image of her mentor as a benevolent leader and to help maintain her mentor's credibility among employees.

> *Pamela*: Some people found that Marta overestimated how quickly things could get done or how cheaply things could get done. And people started to come to me and say, "Is that true? Can you really produce this report in this amount of time?" But I respected Marta and I always followed through on what she said even if I disagreed with her. There were times when I was horrified at some of things that she asked for—I felt that it put me in a really tough spot. Once I had to tell staff they were going to have to work late on a Friday night to get something done because Marta promised it without checking to see if we could do it first.
>
> It was very embarrassing and difficult for me. But I had this sense of obligation to her because—she always came through on a personal level for me. When she said she was going to get me a promotion, she did. When she said she was going to get me a raise, she did. So, I felt a sense of loyalty to her. I still do.

Part of what we hear in Pamela's account is that not only could she be trusted to mobilize her department to complete an impossibly high volume of work under very tight deadlines—she was also willing to perform an emotional service for her mentor by hiding the fact that it was Marta, not her, who had burdened employees with unrealistic work demands.

One of the most common roles for protégés to play is the *good listener*, providing a trusty sounding board and repository for the mentor's troublesome feelings. In these interactions, mentors feel safe to express frustrations, denounce the organization, question directives from superordinates, and come to depend on protégés as confidantes.

> *Penny:* Marge had a need for someone in the workplace to relate to on a personal level . . . There was an insane amount of work and incredible stress attendant to it . . . She definitely wants an ally. I'm sure she really wanted somebody whose loyalty could not be questioned . . .
>
> *Bonnie:* What do you think Marge gets from knowing you?
>
> *Penny:* An ear. A really discreet ear.

By observing and listening, protégés become extremely attuned to the smallest details of their mentors' personalities. They learn to read them astutely—their likes, dislikes, hot buttons, mood swings, pet peeves, etc. Sensitized by this knowledge, protégés work around these things—for example, by avoiding touchy subjects, ignoring eccentricities, rationalizing capricious behaviors, or by denying the mentor's weaknesses or vulnerabilities. Hence, in the *diverter* role, the protégé cultivates and uses emotional radar to help move attention away from the mentor's foibles. In some cases, diversion is used to cover up for the mentor. One example is a regional manager who was willing to act out the part of a "ditzy" protégé in order to play up an image of her mentor as the "stoic," and as "tough as nails." In so doing, she protected the mentor from owning up to her own frailties; yet this was at the expense of the protégé who had to downplay her own competency and repute as a serious contender in their company.

In contrast to the general sociological view that the performance of this kind of emotional labor is onerous, my conversations show that protégés seem to find pleasure in the loyalty rituals. Especially as they look back on the early years in the relationship, protégés' stories reflect eagerness, pride, and playfulness in carrying out both material and emotion work for the mentor. They seem to welcome the opportunity to show appreciation and identify themselves as standing with the mentor by "doing for" them. As it happens, carrying out much of this emotion work actually affords protégés a measure of control and influence as they safeguard information shared by mentors in confidence, counsel others about how to most effectively approach the mentor, provide relief and support to the mentor under stress, and hone an emotional understanding about how to relate to and manage the space around the mentor. Through these acts of emotional catering, protégés carve out a niche of utility and a deep affinity to mentors and in the process attempt to satisfy the condition of reciprocity in the loyalty. This is often a satisfying way to pay the mentor back.

Nevertheless, even as protégés might seem to pull the strings of their own loyalty enactments, they do not always do so without reservation. As relationships progress, loyalty demands on protégés evoke mixed feelings including doubt about the need for them to play out such roles, fear of reprisal for competing with or succeeding the mentor, anxiety about and wishes for separation, and envy of the mentor's power. Hence, even though Patsy was content to do the clean-up work for Melissa, over time she began to worry about trying to chart her own course as a novelist as if cultivating her own style might be construed as a betrayal of her mentor. Penny was flattered to have her mentor count on her as a confidante but her eager attitude gave way to frustration and an upsetting sense of inequity as she came to feel there was little airtime for *her* in the relationship. And while Pamela felt compelled to cover for Marta's overload of work—allowing her mentor to remain the "good-cop" in their good-cop–bad-cop duo—she disappointed herself by "sitting on" grievances about her mentor's seemingly arbitrary demands. Each conflict and compromise underscored the connection and constraint brought on by the goal of preserving loyalty.

Huddling

Creating a boundary around the pair to show loyalty also has ritualistic qualities. The most common methods I have heard mentors and protégés use to act this out are entrusting each other with secrets and banding together in opposition to a third party. Picking up on oedipal themes, interactions like these—as suggested earlier in this chapter—help to create and maintain the sense of exclusivity between mentors and protégés; the primary group sensibility (the "we-ness") both reflects and reaffirms their loyal ties. That said, the process of accentuating the pair's boundaries need not be public. While there may be official or widely shared recognition of the mentor–protégé alliance in an organization, often it is only the mentor and protégé who are aware of the collusive boundary marking and loyalty affirming processes described here. In what follows, that is, I will not be referring to whether other people in a professional network or organization are aware of a pair's mentorship; rather I will be addressing the ways in which mentors and protégés use exclusion or repudiation of others to play up their fidelity to each other.

Bonnie: You're saying that she knew she could count on you fairly early on?

Polina: Yes, yes.

Bonnie: What is it about you that she was picking up on?

Polina: Well, the loyalty—that's number one.

Bonnie: But how would she know that?

Polina: I think she tested me over time. I think she would tell me things in confidence and see if they came back to her.

Bonnie: Did she tell you not to share them with anybody else?

Polina: No, because I knew. I'm smart. I know what is being told in confidence. One signal we always had was when she had something to tell me in confidence, she wouldn't say, "this is confidential." She'd say "close the door." And when I'd get up and close the door, I knew—it was like an unspoken rule—this doesn't leave this office. And I never broke that.

Sharing secrets at once solidifies and tests loyalty as it tethers mentors and protégés into a commitment of restraint; parties agree to withhold the content of the secret from others. Keeping the secret confirms allegiance, but it does so as Simmel (1950) sharply observed, only because the chance to expose it and thus to betray the other are resisted:

> The secret . . . is full of the consciousness that it *can* be betrayed; that one holds the power of surprises, turns of fate, joy, destruction—if only, perhaps of self-destruction. For this reason, the secret is surrounded by the possibility and temptation of betrayal . . . The secret puts a barrier between men but, at the same time, it creates the tempting challenge to break through it, by gossip or confession. (pp. 333–334)

The word secret comes from the French root *secernere*, which means to separate, distinguish, or set apart. Drawing lines around who gets to know the secret and who does not inflates its value; by necessitating that others are excluded from knowing the secret, the information seems all the more dear and parties privy to it—for good or for bad—feel special. Nevertheless, being expected to hold secrets in an organizational or professional context can put mentors and protégés in a dreadful bind.

One mentor I spoke to, Manolo, had the wrenching task of having to execute two rounds of layoffs over the time he worked with his protégé, Paulette. Both times the fact that he gave Paulette advance warning of the layoffs was of small comfort to her in that she learned that at least *she* would not be fired. And after five years of working closely together and basically learning the retail business from her mentor, Paulette's loyalty was hard to shake. Still, she felt saddled with unwanted, oppressive details of the retrenchment, given the fact that some of her co-workers were scheduled to be laid off. Being asked to hold the secret pit her colleague friends against her mentor in a test of loyalty.

> *Bonnie*: Did he ask you to hold secrets for him?
>
> *Paulette*: Well, yes—about the first downsizings. I knew who was going to go and I was neither allowed to share the knowledge, obviously with the people who'd be affected nor to let on that I knew.
>
> *Bonnie*: Were you ambivalent about holding that secret?
>
> *Paulette*: Actually—my god, at that point I was *really* ambivalent about it. I was very conflicted. I felt very, very, very guilty toward the people who weren't going to have jobs anymore.

Sadly, the second round of layoffs at the firm occurred between my first and second interview with Paulette. So, when we met for the second interview the ordeal was fresh and the upset about keeping the secret was palpable:

> *Paulette*: A third of our department just lost their jobs. It's been a really traumatic week at work . . . I've had a lot of difficulty coming to terms with it even though I knew it was in the offing . . . Obviously, everybody around me—my colleagues who I have really close relationships with—some of them aren't there anymore. And it's really just been a big huge adjustment for everybody. And a really sad and bitter one at the same time . . . We were a department of twenty-five. We're now a department of fifteen.

Bonnie: Was this a shock to you?

Paulette: It was. I felt the impact as a great shock because . . . just the emotions that were stirred up by it. In point of fact, it was something that Manolo had told me about but no one else. And he told me not so much because it was a function of my job to know as because it was really impossible for him to carry it around by himself. So, I had kind of been repressing the knowledge . . . We were talking about it to a certain extent, privately, before any of this was announced . . . He told me over a month ago . . . I hope and trust that having someone on the scene in the workplace to share the knowledge with did make it somewhat easier for him. It was very strange because one of things that absolutely, obviously, I can't say anywhere at work is that I was privy to this knowledge beforehand. It would put him in a lot of jeopardy. Obviously, my colleagues wouldn't regard me the same way either.

Not all secrets, of course, are so high stakes. One pair, for example, told me about trying to keep *the fact of their mentorship* a secret. The mentor was extremely cautious in her dealings with the protégé so that other employees wouldn't become jealous. She was nervous about how the intensity of her affection and attention towards the protégé would be interpreted by others in the department. Mainly, however, she wanted to avoid a situation she had experienced when she was being mentored decades prior: she did not want to be seen as inseparable from her protégé nor did she want her protégé to be perceived as inseparable from her. Hence, many of their sometimes ten times a day meetings took on the aura of a clandestine affair. They met behind closed doors, and to ensure that there would be no charge of favoritism, the mentor never lunched or socialized with her protégé outside of work.

Bonnie: So the specialness of the relationship wasn't apparent to other people? Do you think it was apparent to Patrice that there was something unique going on here?

Martha: Oh yeah. We would talk about it that way. I would say, "Look, you understand that *this* is different. This is special. This means something more to me."

Bonnie: For example, what would you be pointing out that was special and different?

Martha: I would let her know that within the context of an average relationship, this is how I would handle it and that I'm giving her *more information* because I want her to understand the process and not just the result. And that she had to understand that this was because of the context of our relationship. Our relationship was more intense than most boss and subordinate relationships. And Patrice, yes, she did understand that.

Bonnie: How would she take that?

Martha: She would appreciate it—that's why it continued. She was grateful. I let her know that I was giving her more information than I usually would or when something was happening in the group—it was *she* I would select to share it with so that she could have the input. Because I felt that Patrice's and my thinking on something was the total picture. I didn't need my other two managers to give me the total picture. They were unaware that I had already met with her. She was very good at never indicating that and never going beyond the information that she knew was right for that context. Although between us there was that "there's more to this and we both know it."

The more Martha tried to conceal the mentorship alliance, that is, the more "secret" it became, the more "dear" or precious it evidently seemed to others in the department. Recall my earlier description of loyalty as embodied in the parties' eagerness and riveting emotional attention. Quite predictably, in Patrice's opinion, *this* secret was in fact no secret at all:

Patrice: It was clear that Martha and I were more than just manager and subordinate. You could just sense that about people. I think people knew that. I think that people were—is "jealous" the right word?—that I had that close relationship with her. I'm sure that people were upset that Martha gave me opportunities that they didn't get from their managers. She was protective of me and some managers were not protective of their staff.

Similar to the ways in which secrets are used to create and sustain a dyadic huddle, another way that mentors and protégés close ranks— albeit with more aggression—involves projection, scapegoating, spoiling, or engaging in other kinds of malicious gossip about a third party. In his piercing analysis of the *folie à deux* dynamics between organizational partners, Kets de Vries (1980) sums this process up as "the search for the enemy" (p. 103). The third party can be anyone: most often in the stories I have heard it includes colleagues, managers, executives, or sometimes even company leaders. (I have yet to hear of subordinates or novice professionals as targets of this process.) The main boundary declaring mechanism here involves transmuting the third party into an "other"—someone perceived as different and *lesser* than the pair. Even in instances when the third party is envied (rather than being seen as inferior), the pair engages in spoiling—denying the good the third party may possess. In the process of taking down a third party, the pair affirms their good fortune or sense of superiority and takes pride in the tenacity of their bond. I use the phrase "three to tango" to evoke an image of this dynamic wherein a third party is conscripted into a dance with the mentorship dyad in ways that strengthen the boundary around the pair.

While other individuals are inevitably drawn into boundary defining activity, it is a subtle process and is rarely detected or named. What I mean by *use* of a third party, however, is crucial: *often the third party does not do anything per se to the dyad* but instead serves as a target or repository of the dyad's collusive projections. The mentoring pair may be cognizant of its use of the third party or oblivious to it. They may know that allegiance to the mentorship heats up because of maneuvers against the third party or this impact may go unattributed.

For example, a colleague in the same company department may be cast as an object of mutual dislike. Mentor and protégé may distance themselves from the colleague, gossip about the colleague's alleged or actual flaws, blame the colleague for company or departmental woes, etc. As they do so, they cement their bonds of identification and loyalty—sharing something together (e.g., affirming to themselves that they are smarter, morally superior, on a faster track) that excludes the colleague. The shared quality gives mentor and protégé the feeling that they are in the same two-person boat with one another.

Allegiance was more firmly etched, for example, as Pearl and Miro began to verbalize their common disregard of another manager, Dina—a woman they derided for "bad morals." Pearl lamented, "we both thought it was disgusting that this woman Dina was cheating on her husband." Painting themselves as more virtuous than their allegedly unscrupulous colleague, Pearl remembered her relationship with Miro intensifying:

> *Pearl:* Dina was walking around like she was the Queen Bee when she wasn't. Frankly, Dina was sleeping with clients and she was cheating on her husband. That bothered both of us. And as we realized that neither one of us could stand her and that we had little respect for her, Miro

and Dina's relationship deteriorated. Interestingly, Miro and my relationship stepped up from there.

Similarly, in another case, a clear outline of loyalty began to emerge as mentor and protégé acknowledged their mutual contempt for a colleague. This was a pair—two faculty members at a small liberal arts college in the Midwest—who had had trouble making a good connection with each other at the start of their relationship; the third party unwittingly served as a catalyst to turn this around. The mentor, Max, was a senior colleague—a tenured professor, and the protégé, Perry, was a newly hired junior faculty member. Irena, the third party, was another professor; all three were in the same department.

Part of what's compelling in this case is that the antipathy toward the third party—and all of the ways that this feeling was milked and acted out by the pair—formed the heart of what Fletcher refers to as the "shared history" that lays the foundation of loyalty. That is, the series of interactions and struggles between Max and Perry *about the third party* gave them the chance to wrestle through something together. The following vignette depicting the evolution and indelible emotional influence of the three-to-tango process—draws our attention to the backdoor struggles through which loyalty can be incited in a mentorship.

*   *   *

Case vignette: Loyalty intensifies as mentor and protégé bond in opposition to a third party

Perry felt she had been courted into her new junior faculty position at the college by Max who had been on the search committee but once she actually arrived on campus, she found Max distant and cool. Max admitted to me that he took a few steps back from his initial engagement with Perry. Though he had offered advice to Perry throughout the interview process, he wanted to be prudent about how he proceeded in his relationship with his new junior colleague now that she was hired.

He liked Perry well enough yet from the start he could tell that they were very different sorts. They were in different life and career stages, and their substantive intellectual interests overlapped only superficially. Their politics and backgrounds were vastly different in ways that were crucial to Max and made him cautious. But just as important were the emotional signals. Max was worried that Perry would gobble him up if he made himself too available to befriend her at the beginning.

Perry let her guard down very quickly, and let Max know about how anxious she was about moving to the college town and establishing a new life. Max did not want to be rejecting, but he also wanted to establish a boundary. He offered Perry a listening ear and left it at that. Perry, on the other hand, was very let down when she saw that Max was not about to be her new chum on campus.

Perry: I had the impression that this was a real kind of strong community and that people did a lot of stuff together but when I first got here, I thought that it wasn't like that. It really was a shocker. I was very unhappy here at first.

Bonnie: Did you feel kind of abandoned by Max?

Perry: Totally abandoned. I still don't know what was going on. But later I interpreted it as having to do with Irena, another junior faculty member also in our program—a pretty hateful creature. I didn't know that, of course, when I first came. Irena colonized me when I first got here. She wanted to have dinner all the time, she wanted to do this, she wanted to do that. I was always with her . . .

Bonnie: What did she want from you?

Perry: She wanted me to be her best buddy. She was very isolated and lonely. She'd taken the job and started a year before I did. She already had alienated a fair number of people including Max, pretty substantively.

But I didn't know the politics. I walked into a very hairy political situation. I had no clue.

Although in some ways she was immediately put off by Irena, Perry admitted that she'd succumbed to Kim's "colonization" of her because *she* was lonely and felt abandoned by Max. But it also happened that Irena was Max's nemesis.

Max: Perry was here for six or seven months before we ever had a conversation about Irena. I had my own feelings about Irena that were quite negative. But it's not wise to share those especially with junior people . . . But you got to feel like she'll figure it out . . . When Perry came—I didn't know if she was going to be discreet or not. But given my experience, I had to err on the side of "Do not talk to her about the fact that this woman is a horrible bitch" because before you know it, six people could know what you think about this woman. And that would be real bad. So, no I didn't—I tried to be available. I knew that at some point Perry was going to figure out that Irena tries to dump work on everyone else and is *bad news*.

This was the chief reason, then, that Max kept Perry at arm's length. He did not trust Irena personally nor did he respect her as a faculty member. He wanted to warn Perry about Irena's habit of trying to off load work to other faculty members but decided it was better to wait to see if Perry came to him first. He didn't feel he knew Perry well enough to give her the low down on Irena and wasn't sure he could trust Perry, especially if it turned out that his own contempt for Irena was divulged. Newcastle was a small college and when one made a life there, certain dissatisfactions had to be tolerated. Perry sensed Max's ambivalence about opening up to her about Irena:

Perry: Max took me out to lunch the second week of classes. I think he wanted to kind of let me in on the fact that Irena wasn't okay. But he didn't trust me and so he kept it very close to the vest. So I got taken out to lunch in this very conspiratorial way and then wasn't told anything. That made me even more confused.

Max's hunch was right—that at some point Perry would finally get fed up with Irena and see the light on her own—probably at the point at which *she* had been exploited by her. Then they would talk.

Perry: Irena is the kind of person who'd tell a student that . . . she "had no integrity" and that she "didn't know how her friends thought of her" and that she "was entirely thoughtless and irresponsible and selfish" because she got a paper in late . . . You know, she's just—she's a mean person in a lot of ways. Just mean. She treats people in a way that I wouldn't treat my dog.

. . . I think the break in my relationship with Irena and my break in my relationship with Max was when I called Max and said, "What am I going to do about this woman?" She'd just talked to the secretary in a way that was so amazingly demeaning that I couldn't bear it. I couldn't stand it. She had the office next to mine and she would kind of lean on my door and treat me . . . as if I agreed with how she was handling it. And she would treat this woman with so much disrespect it was really . . .

Bonnie: So was it like you were guilty by association?

Perry: Yeah—I mean I just . . . I got allied with her and I—you know— didn't realize what was happening . . .

Bonnie: Was she trying to pull you away from Max and . . .

Perry: Yes. She kind of talked trash to me about Max . . .

Bonnie: What a way to come into a job!

Perry: God it was horrible.

After the first semester, Perry began to seek out advice from Max about how to handle Irena:

Perry: Max is the one who told me that Irena didn't have as much control over me as I thought. He would say, "Just ignore her." Actually I would call Max if there was some kind of shit that Irena was trying to pull on me. And I'm the junior member of the program. Irena would really try to get me to do a lot of her work. And in fact, she did get me to do a lot of her work. I mean this fourth class I'm teaching, for example, should not have been mine to teach. It should have been Irena's. So I would call Max for that directly . . .

Apparently amused by the recollection, Max chuckled as he recalled the times Perry fled to his office to "bitch" about Irena:

Max: She didn't want to do it in *her* office. She would come in here to escape sometimes . . . Just get away, you know? And my office is kind of like a little kid clubhouse . . . tucked away here in the woods.

Remembering it as a turning point in the mentorship—a time in which she was finally able to profess her loyalty to her mentor, Perry described a daring exchange she had with Max in which the full breadth of their mutual aversion to Irena was revealed.

Chock with symbolic meaning, Perry showed Max a letter she'd written to oppose Irena's tenure. Writing the letter reflected something gutsy about herself that she felt Max was finally able to recognize—that she was worthy of liking, and was not all that bad just because they didn't share the same politics. Perry could prove to Max in this bold act that she had the mettle to speak out against injustice and thus, align with him.

Perry: I think that he decided at that point that at least I might have a good heart . . . I showed him my letter and I asked for his help. I said, "This is what I think I'm going to send. Do you think this is smart?

. . . I laid my cards on the table. This is what I think. It was kind of my first political act . . . It was not a favorable letter . . .

Bonnie: What was his advice?

Perry: Max is not at all supportive of Irena. In fact, to some degree I felt like Max and I have gotten closer together over our condemnation of

Irena—which troubles me sometimes because I don't think that's a great basis for—but it's not obviously everything that goes on. I just decided I didn't want to think about Irena anymore—one way or the other.

From that time forward, the drama that evolved in relation to the third party became something like a joint cause—something for Max and Perry to rally their relationship around. It became a point of reference—a clear marker for the pair to establish that they were on the same side—a relational base that had been precarious. Yet, it did not escape Perry's notice that this pivot point—mutual contempt of a colleague—might be a weak foundation to hold a relationship together. And she never did feel completely secure in Max's regard for her, independent of his feelings for Irena. Still smarting from this when we met to talk about the mentorship, she described this fact as dogging her connection with Max for many years to come.

*   *   *

Final thoughts

In wrapping up this chapter, a few implications from the analysis of mentor–protégé loyalty warrant final emphasis. The first deals with the nature of loyalty as an emotion that holds a relationship together. The illustrations presented vividly show that there are positive and negative aspects to the emotional grip that mentorship loyalty has, but most importantly that these aspects are dialectical. Loyalty is an essential ingredient in moving the mentor and protégé to develop and want to sustain their identity as a pair. The "we" feeling that evolves feels good. The sense of communion enriches the lives of mentor and protégé as they come to care about, extend themselves for, and protect one another. And the help that the parties offer to each other in the name of loyalty—on very practical as well as professional and sometimes deeply personal matters—is significant. The evidence is strong that a good deal of what mentors and protégés do for one another emanates from loyalty—whether driven by the sense of obligation, self-interest, affection, or a combination of all three.

The fact that mentorship loyalty manifests in the "doing" is a key and novel finding. Conceptually, it moves loyalty beyond the realm of emotion to a social experience entailing relational activity. That is to say, loyalty is a practice as much as it is an emotion. And because of the emotional, strategic, and normative stakes—the pleasures of security, the fears of disappointment, the hunger for status, the desire to succeed, the injunctions from conscience to do what's right, owed, or expected—the practice of loyalty calls out for dramatization and ritual. Mentor and protégé must prove loyalty—it is not sufficient to merely verbalize this. There is a show involved; for the most part, therefore, loyalty is public. Thus any inquiry into mentorship loyalty (or perhaps interpersonal loyalty of any kind for that matter) must pay attention not only to sentiment and intention—that is, whether a person feels or is determined to be loyal towards another—but must factor in behavior, action, and the symbolic value of what one "does" for the other.

While creating a cocoon of trust and enhancing the conditions for creative and at times impassioned collaboration, we see that loyalty also curbs freedom. In its hold, mentors and protégés feel less free to stray, walk away, or turn their backs on commitments. The safety net created by loyalty runs the risk of suppressing voice. Parties feel inhibited to speak their minds—especially to criticize the other or express dissenting opinions when they depend upon the other for protection and support. Pressing for solidarity and exclusivity, loyalty can also lead parties to limit opportunities for meaningful connections with colleagues who could potentially lure them away from the dyadic huddle. In extreme cases, parties may become insulated from important input from other people, ideas can become stale, and jealousy and gossip may be provoked among colleagues. Further, there can be a loss of individual identity as the pair defines itself and comes to be perceived by others as an inseparable duo. One could say that by generating "we-ness," loyalty can also threaten to submerge "me-ness." Individual difference and distinctiveness could be squelched.

Hence, the build-up of loyalty that drives mentor and protégé to go to great lengths to boost each other's careers can also blind them from seeing each other's flaws, stymie the development of independent thought and result in cloning, create dilemmas about whether to pursue challenging opportunities that could distance parties organizationally or philosophically, and lead to sacrifices that sabotage careers. There is no way to be in a loyalty dynamic without debt or reins on freedom. The case of mentorship depicted here illuminates the force that loyalty has in establishing and sustaining conditions and expectations for reciprocity and sacrifice in intimate relationships. Disloyalty is not the only risk that loyalty carries: loyalty itself is risky.

Clearly such risks are higher for protégés than for mentors because of the authority and dependency relation. That the protégé is more vulnerable to loyalty's constraints—politically and in the material sense—is evidenced in this exploration. Particularly when the mentor is a direct supervisor or boss, the protégé risks loss of stature, promotion and retention opportunities, and access to preferred assignments and powerful networks. At the same time, though they owe more, protégés *have* less to give back—in the conventional sense, that is—and they compensate for this inequality by enacting loyalty toward mentors symbolically through emotional caretaking and deferential acts of material labor. While most regard this as part of the implicit contract and are sanguine about the ritualized performances of loyalty, tensions in this area are likely to arise as protégés mature in their organizational and professional identities. Loyalty will be peppered with resentment if protégés are not given the space to grow out of the assistant role or service orientation towards mentors.

Whatever the protégé's positional disadvantage, there is no question that the dialectic in loyalty imperils the mentor as well. In long-term relationships it does not seem any easier for mentors than it is for protégés, emotionally speaking, to distance themselves or breach the alliance—even when remaining loyal entails substantial sacrifice or exposure. Mentorship carries political and reputational risks; in some ways the stakes can be higher for the mentor who, depending upon his or her professional biography, may in fact have more to lose. As they stick by one another, mentors and protégés wrestle with these issues.

While loyalty binds mentors and protégés in allegiances that can at times become too confining for its own good, generativity is a process that involves imagining what sticks to the partners after they separate. The next chapter explores questions about what is passed on in mentorship, how this occurs, and why ambivalent wishes and fears are stirred up by this process.

CHAPTER FIVE

The anxieties of influence: generativity in mentorship

Generativity involves making an imprint on another person as a form of legacy. It is crucial to look closely at this process as it captures a large part of the motivation to mentor. At core is the desire to transcend one's individual existence. That is, mentors wish to give something of themselves to protégés in order to extend their ideas, values, beliefs, professional acumen, and ways of being into the future. This can serve as an expression of the mentor's purpose and potency—a sense that what he or she knows and has accomplished has made a mark on the world. Sometimes that mark is very literal, such as when mentors "dot their networks with people who grew up under them," to use a phrase of one executive I spoke with—using generativity to pave the way for succession.

While it can have concrete manifestations—such as training a protégé in a specific skill, giving practical advice about personal or professional aspirations, or preparing the protégé to take over one's job—generative activity tends to be elusive. Often it is unseen, woven into the fabric of routine interactions between mentors and protégés. Moreover, what exactly the mentor wishes to impart, how he or she goes about doing so, and how and what the protégé takes in from the process are not usually mapped out in advance, nor do they always leave an observable imprint. It is not unusual for protégés to talk about something ineffable that has happened to them as a result of knowing their mentor—some indescribable way in which their lives were lifted by the mentorship experience. And it is also not uncommon for either party—mentor or protégé—not to know when the influence took hold or what acts lead to the imprint. For Pelota, her mentor's effect seemed almost ethereal,

> *Pelota*: Anybody who comes in contact with [my mentor] will be changed because . . . gosh, I don't how to say all this stuff without sounding really corny. She's just really unique! I mean she's like fresh air. Like just meeting her is like, I don't know—like a first spring or something—just something fresh.

Similar to my framing of idealization and loyalty, I will explore generativity as a mode of attachment—a way of connecting one person to another. That said, as noted in the introduction, one key feature that distinguishes these processes is that they each link to a different time referent. While the attachment in idealization is energized by imagos from the past—particularly ones that originate from early childhood fantasies of parental omnipotence—and loyalty anchors its bond in contemporary everyday interactions, the ties of generativity are clearly oriented toward the future. Mentors project parts of their lives and the traditions and ideals they stand for into the future through interactions with protégés who internalize these parts with the hope that someday the latter may in turn pass them on to others. Taking in the mentor's experience and talents constitutes a feeding for the protégé. Still, while the process can be deeply nourishing, conversations with both mentors and protégés suggest that generative activity can also be surprisingly disappointing, conflict-laden, and even depleting. My aim in this chapter is to shed light on the ways that mixed feelings like these are intrinsic to and produced by this process.

Influence

Generativity encompasses a distinct kind of influence—one which whether or not the mentor intends for it—leaves an imprint on the protégé and whether or not the protégé acknowledges it has the signature of the mentor. This is an elaboration of Harold Bloom's weighty insight in *The Anxiety of Influence* (1973), a book in which the urge to be original is explored in the context of unconscious appropriation between poets and their predecessors. Bloom forcefully argues that no matter how much we might strive to create something wholly original, something that comes from a pure solitary creative impulse, we cannot escape influence from teachers and forbearers. That is also to say that we cannot exist outside of history or culture.

Although it is suffused with authority dynamics, generativity does not concern the bureaucratic type of influence. Training a protégé because it is mandated as part of one's job as supervisor is not itself an example of generativity. To be generative, the act must come from personal motivation. John Kotre (1996) captures the essence of this personal interest as "a desire to invest one's substance in forms of life and work that will outlive the self" (p. 10). An act becomes generative he writes, "only when it is imbued with the sense of extending oneself into the apprentice or attaching oneself to a lasting art" (p. 13). Be that as it may, generative influence does not necessarily unfold consciously on the part of the mentor. Sometimes the mentor is unaware of his or her wish to influence, defends against it, or does not grasp how much impact he or she has on the protégé. Sometimes, as alluded to above and as we will see in case illustrations later in the chapter, the mentor struggles with the boundaries of his or her influence, and may be anxious about losing control over that which is passed on to the protégé or, for some, about being given too much control in this process.

Just as I have explored the contradictory nature of idealization and loyalty in mentorship, so too should we approach generative influence as ambivalent—at once vital and risky. While the mentor's influence can be altruistic—leading to satisfying professional and personal development for a protégé, or communal—aimed at making positive contributions to a professional community writ large, it can also be narcissistic—self-serving for the mentor and in some cases, exploitative of the protégé. When protégés are used primarily as receptacles for immortalizing the mentor's achievements or teachings, generative influence can stunt rather than promote individual growth and cultural enrichment. And although it probably goes without saying—not everything deserves to be passed on. Indeed, some may take solace in the fact that a harmful trend is *not transmitted*. "This ends here," says the mentor who, acting as a buffer, decides to stop a pattern (e.g., professional hazing) that has caused suffering.

In the chapter sections to follow, I will unpack the various dimensions of generative influence identified above, calling attention to the ambivalence that attends each.

Generative objects

If generativity entails "kissing and biting the hand that feeds," to use Jessica Benjamin's (1995) tart phrase, John Kotre (1996) surely has done so by critiquing and reworking the conception of generativity put forth by his intellectual mentor, Erik Erikson. Instead of seeing it as a developmental response to midlife crisis as Erikson did, Kotre argues that generativity is an urge that seeks expression throughout the life cycle in four different forms: biological, parental, technical, and cultural. Each type confers its own kind of generative "objects"— that is, the substance of the influence—the stuff that is being passed on. Because they are most applicable to mentorship, I am mainly interested in the latter two types—technical and cultural. I also identify and discuss a third type—"political generativity" because of its direct relevance to mentoring. (See Figure 5.1)

Mentors are technically generative when they pass on skill, knowledge, craft, or technique; the mentor who is culturally generative goes beyond teaching in the technical sense. He or she offers lessons on the meaning and values that set the stage for a protégé to prudently use the skills and knowledge, and shares ideas about how that knowledge fits into the larger social world, how it enriches a life, and how it contributes to culture. Hence, technical generativity concerns *how to do something* and *what one needs to know to do that thing*. It is about information and practice. Cultural generativity, on the other hand, concerns significance—*what that something means*. It is about insight and integration. Technical and cultural generativity apply to human relations broadly, while political generativity—a category I am adding to Kotre's scheme—is relevant to professional mentorship specifically. It involves passing on power, networks, position, clout, and responsibility—typically, though not exclusively, associated with succession.

Clearly, the three types of generativity overlap. When helping a protégé navigate organizational politics by giving advice about which

TYPES AND OBJECTS OF MENTORSHIP GENERATIVITY	
Types	**Objects**
Technical	**Practical-utilitarian**
Concerns how to do things (skill) and what to know (substantive knowledge)	Information, skill, technique, craft, and facts
Cultural	**Cultural-historical**
Concerns what things mean (significance) and how to be (one's place in the world)	Insight, traditions, values, meanings (the total picture/gestalt)
	Cultural-psychological
	Identity, character, vocational and life purpose
Political	**Political-succession**
Concerns the nuts and bolts skill and knowledge to ascend and the meaning and deportment linked to the role of successor	Position, status, power, access to resources, exclusive network

Figure 5.1

colleagues and executives he or she needs to avoid, flatter, coddle, confront, etc., the mentor not only offers practical information about how to finesse interactions with selected individuals in present day situations, but also helps the protégé build relationship capital that will facilitate good career moves down the line. Interwoven throughout these processes, the mentor tells stories to protégés—interpretive sketches of work life, often touching on the history and culture of their shared organization or field—and he or she reflects on what it means to carry oneself as a professional. Such guidance instills protégés with a larger sense of purpose relative to the fields or companies in which they work, as well as a greater appreciation of the impact they could have in their adult lives in general.

Daniel Levinson (Levinson et al., 1978) was especially attuned to this last point—highlighting the expansive reach of the mentor's guidance. One of few writers on mentoring to see the nexus between the personal, professional, and wider cultural significance of the relationship, Levinson depicted mentors as setting an example of how one can live a satisfying life as an adult—something more related to addressing existential questions of identity, character, and purpose in the world than to any specific professional or personal pursuit. From this vantage point, a mentor's generative offering involves helping the protégé envision *what kind of person* he or she could become. This framing helped me make sense of the breadth of a mentor's influence that I heard often in protégé accounts. Pierette, a thirty-three-year-old sculptor, for example, told me she carried her mentor's legacy by "becoming much more New York" as a result of their working and socializing together. What rubbed off on her, she said, had to do with fitting into the art world by evolving an "urban sensibility" of which her mentor was apparently a supreme example. Pierette's reflections affirm that mentors serve as models not just related to work but to life more generally—as people whose lives offer templates for protégés to think about and try on for size as part of a process of imagining and crystallizing their own identities and futures.

One might ask how such a conception demonstrates an appreciation for the role of culture in generativity. Key to answering this is to recognize that identity and questions about *how to be* are linked not only to one's personal life but are steeped in cultural meaning as well. While helping the protégé figure out how to be, the mentor conveys ideas about life that may reinforce or in some instances go against culturally accepted beliefs, values, customs, ethics, and standards regarding things like success, pleasure, ambition, work and family balance, integrity, credible authority, a job well done, what it means to be a good woman or man, etc. Thus, how to be, while deeply individual and existential, is also ineluctably a cultural matter set in time and place.

In one mentor's account, we hear about the influence of her own mentor many years prior on how to be as an artist—an intergenerational lesson that she is intent on passing on to her protégé:

> *Meredith:* In retrospect, what it feels like was most important—if I think of the person I was at age twenty or twenty-five—was the emotional support for sustaining failure, for telling me that it's okay to be bad at this. It's part of your job to be bad at this. You're *succeeding* if you feel like you're being bad at this. This allowed me to have the confidence to sit with my sense of inadequacy—to know that its normal . . . In fact, I can say that twenty-five years later—starting a piece, I feel incompetent and non-functional and like I don't know what I'm doing. The only difference is that now I'm comfortable with that feeling . . . its sustainable . . . It doesn't make me terrified and anxious even though it still doesn't feel very good. And when I see Pippa, I always come back to this place to pass that bit of wisdom forward.

Meredith relates here that her mentor's lessons were soothing and indelible—they reassured her years ago and still today that cultural ideals about being expert at one's work obscure the messier parts of the creative process. As Meredith conveyed the importance of adopting a more patient attitude toward oneself—encouraging her protégé to accept feelings of confusion and frustration as a normal part of the process of creativity—she was also making a statement about wanting to leave her mark on culture by making sure to help the next generation resist unrealistic and ultimately inhibiting images of artistic success.

A final type of generative object that emerged in my research involved the political act of handing down a resource invested with power, normally associated with succession. Sometimes the object transferred by the mentor is his or her position in the organization or professional field. As mentors move up or out of their official positions, some will groom protégés to assume the role they are vacating. Even when there is no official position, mentors may aim to convey their status as a respected advisor in a field. Symbolically, they pass the torch to the protégé as a representative of the next generation to assume the mantle of authority, privilege, and responsibility. That said, given changes in the postindustrial work world that are leading many to have less stable and less linear careers, the idea of succession from mentor to protégé is obviously much more complicated. I will delve further into these issues later in the chapter.

Internalization

Protégés, of course, do not swallow whole what their mentors offer. In theory, though generativity could inch towards cloning—turning professional development into something like a rote, two-dimensional process of copying one's mentor—agency and emotional tensions are invariably implicated in and stir up the process. That is, protégés are to some extent mindful of and selective about what they identify with and try to adopt from the mentor. At the same time, owing to psycho-dynamic, social, and cultural prohibitions, they may also try to distance themselves from and try to negate the mentors' influence. What is taken in gets metabolized through filters of conscious and unconscious meanings gleaned from the protégé's life experience, situational and professional context, and a backdrop of societal norms and cultural codes.

For one thing, a protégé's desire and openness to be influenced by and learn from a mentor may be restrained because of taboos over the idea of accepting help. The "I did it on my own" and "I pulled myself up by my bootstraps" ethos, so valorized in American culture inhibits those who wish to receive guidance. Moreover, possessiveness of knowledge (e.g., "that was *my* idea") and priority (e.g., "I had that idea *first*")—two dominant values rooted in individualism—conflict with the pleasure in sharing and the communal process of creation that is part of generativity. Protégés may be less receptive, that is, to a mentor's influence because of pressures like these to be self-made and original. Similarly, a protégé may disavow a mentor's influence because of feeling ashamed of dependency longings that surface during the learning process. I have also met protégés who held them-selves back from generative engagement in order to avoid experienc-ing their own aggression, provoked by envy of what the mentor possessed and they felt they lacked. All of that said, the filters on protégé internalization clearly have many strains that can work against the mentor's generative efforts. Yet not all are as potentially self-defeating as the ones just described. On the positive side are developmental filters, or perhaps better thought of as pushes, that draw protégés not so much away from mentor influence but toward something else. In other words, rather than react defensively, protégés may decline a mentor's influence out of a healthy desire for auton-omy—that is, to distinguish themselves as individuals on a separate course from mentors.

The fact that mentor and protégé are unique individuals inevitably leads to differences in how generative material is donned. When a protégé adopts some aspect of the mentor's style of working, for example, this will inevitably look different on the protégé than on the mentor. Although my point here may seem elementary, it is significant because it underscores the fact that what gets passed on in mentorship is *always transformed*. Internalization, that is, needs to be understood as a process by which the stuff of generativity undergoes this change.

Inhibitors

Like their protégés, mentors are also conflicted about and feel pulled away from wholehearted engagement in generativity. Though it provides them with an enriching sense of personal and professional satisfaction and can offer instrumental rewards such as increased political clout and spread of influence, generativity entails loss. In the act of sharing knowledge, skill, life philosophies, values, etc., the mentor gives up a piece of him or herself. In a sense, mentors surren-der their convictions and most passionately held ideas by making them available for internalization and thus interpretation and trans-formation by someone else. They lose control, that is, over their "precious substance and objects" (Kotre, 1996). The hope, of course, is that the protégé will elaborate in a good way whatever is taken from the mentor. But there is also the risk that the protégé will twist or misrepresent these things.

Moreover, on some level, mentors are aware that protégés could become competitors—using what they have gained from mentors against them. Here, the sense of loss may be experienced with hostility as a threat, a theft, or a betrayal. Sometimes mentors find themselves treading a delicate course, aware of the risk of undercutting themselves as they prepare protégés to replace them. To make a detour around this bind, some take pre-emptive steps by scaling back generative efforts. The "Salieri phenomenon" (Lorber, 1984) captures this well. Named for the Court composer who kept the genius of his protégé, Mozart, from being publicly recognized, Salieri withheld efforts to showcase Mozart to his extensive network of patrons. In so doing, he jealously subverted the opportunity to be generative in order to prevent the outstanding work of his protégé from receiving just acclaim.

Even in the most benign of circumstances, the sense of loss, or even the anticipation of it, is experienced as bittersweet as the protégé's promise is an indelible reminder of the mentor's inevitable obsolescence and mortality. Mentors can become defensive as protégés find their footing in ways that could upstage them. Percy experienced this directly from his mentor and was puzzled and hurt by it. An emerging poet beginning to gain some attention in local circles, he recalled a number of stinging conversations he'd had with his mentor, Marion, a well-regarded professor in the Creative Writing department at their Brooklyn-based college.

> *Percy*: I keep running into Maurice Manning at readings I've been going to. I remember once, when I went to one of his seminars, all the attendees gushed over his work. He's pretty famous—one of the finalists for the Pulitzer prize in poetry a few years ago. Anyway, so he knows me a little bit too . . . he liked the work that I turned in during a Caldera residency I took with him a couple of years ago. So, whenever we see each other, he's really friendly.
>
> *Bonnie*: Does Marion know him?
>
> *Percy*: Sure—everyone does, but that's the thing. A few times over the last few months after I ran into him and we'd chatted, I'd mentioned this to Marion. I thought she would be delighted because Manning would be such a good contact for me. Instead, each time, Marion acted like she "forgot" (made air quotes with his fingers) that I knew him and would sarcastically say, "Oh *you* know *him*?"

To Percy, the put-down in his mentor's snarky response spoke volumes about her annoyance over having to deal with a protégé who in her eyes might have been getting too big for his britches.

*   *   *

Mentors occasionally admit to having mixed feelings about the responsibility that comes with generativity. However primordial the desire to pass on the fruits of one's experience, some view it as burdensome as it brings them face to face with their limitations and imperfections. Whether consciously reflected upon or not, generativity taps into doubts about adequacy and competence—about whether mentors measure up to their own or their protégés' ideals of authority and expertise and can deliver on those expectations. Several who worried about whether they deserved to have this kind of influence said to me that they felt like "imposters."

Finally, generativity may be approached reluctantly as mentors recall and vicariously relive the struggles they faced in the course of their own professional development. While they do find pleasure in sharing their skills and talents, I have met mentors who also resent or are dubious about the process if they perceive protégés as acquiring insight, skills, access, and poise too easily. One such mentor, Melissa, the founder of a tech start-up firm, remembered feeling irked by the way it seemed that her protégé could "just slide into" the firm's management tier after she herself had toiled to seed and grow their company from the ground up. Her feeling was "I had to struggle, why shouldn't you?" Mentors can feel inclined to give and withhold—alternating between wanting to pave the way and remove obstacles for protégés to develop professionally, yet recalling—sometimes bitterly and other times with pride—the hard knocks that they faced while building their own careers. This conflict is most acute when protégés act as if they are entitled to professional spoon-feeding from mentors to bypass the pains and struggles of learning—a theme we have discussed earlier. It is not hard to imagine that this dynamic could put a damper on mentor enthusiasm about sharing what they have.

Identification

Up to this point, I have touched on the motivations of mentors to be generative in the broad sense. But I have not yet taken up the question of why a mentor is generative to this or that particular protégé. What is it about particular protégés that propels the generative urge? Does it matter who one's protégé is or does the desire to influence come to a mentor with any protégé? Examining the role of identification in this process will help answer such questions.

Identification is an essential building block of generativity. There needs to be resonance, that is, between a mentor's experiences, interests, and values and those of the protégé. The image of passing something on to a person who can be trusted to make something good of it in the future links to this basic sense of identification—seeing another as like oneself. Obviously, the fact that mentors care about what happens to generative objects suggests that they are not really "freely" offered. There is always an element of self-interest in the giving. With at least a healthy dose of narcissism, therefore, mentors may ask themselves, "do I feel the protégé is like me? Could this person be like me? Does he or she come from a similar place that I do? Does he or she remind me of myself or anyone I admired when I was younger? Will this person reflect well on me in the years ahead?" Mentors who cannot answer yes to any of these questions because they do not feel a sense of similitude in relation to protégés—or cannot imagine the possibility of ever feeling strongly in this way tend to be conflicted about assuming the generative role and as a result, constrict their efforts.

It should be understood that I mean identification here in both the sociological and psychoanalytic senses. In sociological parlance, identification relates to finding something in common with another person typically on the basis of social background factors like class, religion, gender, sexuality, marital or family status, ethnicity, educational background, etc. Or it can refer to the way that one feels a connection to others who share beliefs, world view, attitudes, hobbies, or life philosophies. Sociologists sometimes use the term *homosocial* to denote the tendency for individuals to identify and associate with others from their same group—however loosely defined. In the concise words of Judith Lorber (1979), "like trusts like."

In the psychoanalytical sense, identification assumes more complex shading. From this standpoint, identification is not necessarily based on qualities that are obvious, immediate, or even reality-based. A mentor may feel a strong emotional attraction to a protégé but have only a vague sense of why that is. His or her investment in the protégé's welfare may go beyond the norm for reasons that elude. Such pulls typically stem from identification based on a mixture of real attributes and experiences as well as unconscious fantasies, transference reactions, and qualities projected on to the protégé. These deeper psychological sources of identification animate and organize generative efforts, breathing a sense of urgency and intensity into the process.

Ordinarily, by virtue of the fact that the pair have found their way into a mentorship, there is already some identificatory resonance between the parties. Yet, identifications are not absolute, total, or static. The degree of identification from mentor to protégé tends to be stronger with respect to certain qualities than with others. We see this in how Malena, a forty-eight-year-old borough official, parsed out aspects of her protégé's career situation and personal style that she could relate to and those she could not. Reminiscent of her own difficulties in trying to navigate a career in a male dominated field, Malena was very tuned into Phoebe's hesitancy about how to forge a satisfying professional life as a woman in politics.

> *Malena*: When I was in Maine and was involved in politics, I was something of a public figure . . . I was articulate, I was smart, I was out there, you know? And I'm also warm and friendly and pretty easy to be with. So, it's not hard for me to see why young women would just think that anything they could do to help my campaign would be wonderful. It's always been young women that I have nurtured . . . I've taken that seriously because I have this thing about young men in politics and how they've always got other people taking care of them, watching out for them, setting them up, whatever. I think girls deserve that too, you know? So, I've taken pretty seriously my responsibility to be there for young women.

Malena clearly saw Phoebe as one of the young women she wished to raise in politics. Yet, given her own effusive, spontaneous, activist inclinations, and seat of the pants style, she admitted that she had had trouble identifying with Phoebe's heady, methodical, intellectual, and theoretical bent towards their common work as civic leaders.

> *Malena*: I really admire Phoebe a lot. I think she's really smart and committed to political substance. I mean she's got a very clear political philosophy and perspective that governs where she puts her energy . . .
> I always thought I don't really deserve the name "radical" because that assumes you got a philosophical underpinning and all I had was an emotional response . . . But it was not rational in any way or educated . . . I just had this nose for injustice and wouldn't tolerate it . . . And so, folks I work with would see something they didn't like and they'd bring

it to me and say, "You know, something ought to be done about this," and then the next thing you know, I'd be on it—railing at this rule or that policy . . . I wasn't an intellectual. Not at all.

. . .I feel like Phoebe's really grounded with a political philosophy. She understands it and she knows what she believes and why she believes it. And she can bring that perspective to an analysis of it. Just the broadest range of things come to her. I never thought that I'm very good at that.

One could say that almost by nature, mentor and protégé were attracted to different spheres of the political field. Consequently, while confident that she could offer general career encouragement and regale about her own fight to carve out a place for women in politics, Malena did not feel she had much to offer regarding Phoebe's choices about the substantive areas of work that she might pursue. In this regard, Malena was insecure about the value of her influence as she confessed, "I don't know that I have anything to contribute to Phoebe's development."

Even in the most satisfying and productive mentorships, identifications are ambivalent, partial, and change over time. Just as a mentor and protégé come into the relationship with common backgrounds and proclivities that might predispose them to identify with each other initially, each party is also affected by the other and by the situations they go through together as the mentorship evolves. Events and exchanges that alter perceptions or feelings about the likeness, appeal, sense of camaraderie, mutuality, or shared understandings will have an impact upon identification that in turn will affect generativity. And as relationships progress, mentors may come to view protégés as becoming more like them or as individuals whose capacities to carry on their good name become more evident. It may also be the case that as time goes on, mentors may identify less with protégés. Fantasies about likeness and resonance are subject to testing against real situations and events as the mentorship progresses. Hence, while contoured by biography, identification is a fluid, interactional process—not a fore-ordained *thing*.

(Mis)identifications

There is no doubt that identification is central to energizing a mentor's desire for generativity. At the same time, however, when identifications are built on fragile or faulty foundations based on projections or distorted appraisals of the other, unrealistic expectations and disappointments often follow for mentors and protégés and, as will be illustrated, can wind up misguiding generative efforts.

One problematic pattern comes from over-identification—that is, when mentors see protégés as so much like themselves that judgment about what protégés need and can accept in the way of generative influence becomes clouded. Mentors who over-identify with protégés tend to want to "fix" aspects of their protégés that they find unacceptable in themselves. They risk collapsing likeness with sameness, pushing generativity in the direction of cloning. "Since my protégé is like me, I assume he or she is interested in X, Y, and Z because I can relate to these things." It is easy to see how one could slip into forgetting the subjectivity of the other person when identification and fantasies of narcissistic gratification around that are strong. At the same time, this can lead to frustration and misdirected anger at protégés when attempts to fix or replicate oneself do not take.

Contrasted with over-identification is under-identification—when mentors see protégés as too little like themselves to be entrusted with their generative objects. Mentors who under-identify with protégés distance themselves from generative activity because they fear losing control over their "precious substance"—referred to earlier. This can lead to a generativity stalemate, provoking a fair amount of guilt for the mentor and diluting the mentoring process.

My view is that both types of identification malfunctions reflect narcissistic dilemmas set off in the generativity process. That is, mentors become distressed as they confuse what is for them and what is for the protégé in the relationship. Ultimately, the efficacy of the imprinting process is impaired. The following case illustrations address ambivalence expressed in generativity efforts that stem from the two kinds of problematic identification described above. I should stress that these do not represent the only types of complications that can arise from identification. How identification can strengthen or undermine generative efforts is highly idiosyncratic in terms of how it plays out in particular mentorships.

* * *

*Case vignettes: Generativity difficulties when a mentor
over- or under-identifies with a protégé*

Case 1: We are too much alike

A story that Meena told me during our interview was one about the trouble that her protégé, Pam, was constantly cooking up for herself at work. Paradoxically, it was a kind of trouble that drew Meena into an alliance with her protégé—it clearly made her care about Pam—and at the same time it was something that beleaguered her throughout their relationship. It was a kind of trouble she felt utterly unable to "break Pam out of" despite repeated attempts. Yet at the root of her frustration, Pam's trouble was something Meena admitted to struggling with herself. In seeing unacceptable aspects of herself in Pam, Meena experienced both identification and repudiation.

The basic problem, according to Meena, was that Pam was continually damaging herself professionally by confiding in and gossiping to colleagues with naïve trust. Such behavior was dangerous at a place like Darlington—an expanding enterprise, hungry to promote top producers and heavily invested in fostering competition. It was doubly dangerous for Pam who had been a leader among the sales force almost from the moment she arrived at the company. Pam was the one to beat—everyone knew it.

But while Pam apparently did not understand the politics of envy in her organization, Meena did. Meena believed she understood the subtext of this situation viscerally—that is, she knew that Pam could get eaten alive. To use her words—Pam was like a "poodle in a ring of pit bulls." The reason that Meena understood this was that she too had faced this predicament. Meena spoke of times when she had opened up too much to colleagues, exposed her vulnerabilities, and got bitten.

> *Meena*: We were the same type of person and because of that we butted heads a lot . . . I saw her do a lot of things that I would have done . . . I was trusting my peers and they were turning and stabbing me in the back. And so, I could get angry at her for doing it but I couldn't resolve it in my own relationships . . .

This raw admission revealed part of what made these issues so hot for Meena: she wanted things to be different for Pam. Partly, this was to mask her own sense of helplessness when faced with the same situation. If she could not save herself from the treachery of colleagues, perhaps, at least she could spare Pam from the same fate.

As Meena told me about this, the tone in her voice had an urgency that made her seem exasperated with Pam over this issue, still, even though it was two years since they had worked together at Darlington. The political immaturity was a part of how Pam operated that Meena could never control or tame. She repeatedly warned Pam not to trust colleagues. This became a mantra. But Pam continued to talk and trust. Ergo, almost everything that Pam told colleagues got twisted into stories that wound up reflecting poorly on her. The gossip often got back to Meena but much more consequentially, to Ralph, the company president.

Meena did not seem to grasp that despite her best intentions, her over-identification got in the way of her attempts to be generative. She got so hooked into trying to rid her protégé of this one problem that she missed opportunities to be influential in other areas. She also did not seem to understand that she undermined her generative potency by modeling the very behavior she was trying to erase in Pam. The fact that Meena allowed herself to become entangled in workplace gossip and to communicate in ways that set some colleagues against each other made it difficult for Pam to absorb the seriousness of her mentor's generative lesson. "Do as I do."

Case 2: We are not enough alike

When mentors strain to identify with protégés and cannot envision them as potentially good bearers of their generative gifts—that is, as unable to make something good of their influence, they are reluctant to make the investment. Some downscale generative efforts. Others carefully circumscribe them. One way this occurs, for example, is by narrowing the scope of generativity to technical or concrete matters, while steering clear of the riskier business of cultural generativity that entails influence on deeper, necessarily more ambiguous questions of meaning, value, and identity.

This type of generative contraction was evident in the mentorship of college sociology professors, Merritt and Parker. The fact that Merritt did not see eye to eye with Parker made it very difficult for him to imagine that his protégé could carry his seed into the future fruitfully. Quite painful was that Parker really wanted to have a chance at it. As Merritt saw it, however, there was a basic divide between himself and Parker that could not be bridged. He spent a good deal of time during our interview talking about all kinds of differences he felt he had with Parker. For one thing, there was the age and generational difference. He was a half generation older and referred to the distinctive eras they grew up in as producing understandings of the world that set them apart.

Merritt: We're really of a different generation actually because kids who grew up in the 1960s and early 70s are way different than those who grew up in the 80s. Different life . . . I perpetually have this vision of Parker as somebody wet behind the ears. I feel like, "Oh my god, she's so young! How could she not know *that?*" . . .

Yet later in our chat, Merritt hinted at a deeper truth—that it was probably not the age difference that mattered so much:

. . .If we were the same age and at the same stage in life, we might not be friends at all. I don't think we'd dislike each other. But we're pretty different.

I sensed that Merritt was searching during our interview for a way to explain why he lacked generative desire with Parker. He seemed to know that generativity was expected of him yet he was resistant to fill this role. That's the part he seemed hung up on. The crux of the conflict—at least as I understood it—was that Merritt worried that because he and Parker held divergent ideological and political perspectives—his generative energies would be wasted. Merritt was a staunch, some might call orthodox Marxist, while Parker was still forming her political identity—more inclined to vogue post-modern viewpoints—yet not at all sure she was ready to declare herself to be part of any "camp":

Merritt: Parker said to me once she doesn't really understand Marxist thinking very well. So, she said, "You really have to tell me about your experience with the old guard"—which I never was associated with because that was a generation earlier! There was no way I was going to go through that with her. No way. I know she wouldn't understand it . . . I don't want to do it just for somebody who admires me intellectually.

Ideological kinship was crucial to Merritt. He classified allies and non-allies on the basis of the schools of thought they aligned with:

Merritt: Frankly when I meet a new person—if I'm really going to get to know them, I have to feel out their world view. It's as if I really don't know who they are unless I can place them socially, historically, and ideologically . . .

. . .People who share my perspective—I don't have to explain anything to them. They already know. I can make little jokes to them and they're not going to take offense. They get the joke. And I can really trust their intellectual judgment. I can't do that with Parker . . . Though she *is* nice. And if she weren't nice, if I didn't think, "Oh this is somebody who deserves a good turn" I never would have mentored her.

Merritt's sentiment, though harsh, came through to Parker loud and clear:

Parker: I don't think he's going to build bridges with people who aren't in places he wants to go . . . I'm not sure where I fit into that . . . Well, I think that he thinks of me as a well-meaning, good-hearted person . . . a wanna-be Marxist. And that's better than a lot of other people here. I'm kind of green behind the ears. It's true enough. You know, Merritt instantly figures people out and he puts them in a catalogue, in a file.

Merritt recalled only one time when he had more than a few minute conversation with Parker about her academic research and writing even though substantive intellectual interaction about one's research routinely forms the heart of academic mentorships. Even conversations about teaching were strained by their differences. Giving a flavor of the kind of tension in their exchanges, Merritt described an encounter in which Parker came to him for advice about what books to use in a course. Merritt said that when *he* teaches the same course, he focuses on classic Marxist texts. But since Parker has been assigned to teach the course, he added with an edge of disgust, "there's none of that now."

Merritt: I could say . . . "Marx wrote some interesting things about human need and commodification—you might want to use those texts. It's sort of easy to understand, it makes students think twice about this and that . . ." But to some degree it's just not going to register. We don't speak the same language or think the same way. So, there's no reason for me to try to win her over. I will not try to win her over.

Apparently allergic to divergent world views, it was quite obvious to me that Merritt did not want to mix intellectually with Parker; he was unable to trust that their basic intellectual stances could merge, mix, or season each other. He didn't want his own ideas sullied by someone who might not "get it" or even worse, get it and do something corrupt with it.

Merritt: You say to somebody. "Look at it this way." It doesn't take. And (snaps his fingers) the next day, they forgot it. Or you hear them repeating it but they don't get it. I don't like that.

Evidently, Merritt shut down the whole arena of generative influence because he felt he could not control the outcome of the process, apprehensive that Parker's internalization and elaboration of his generative object would spoil its original intent.

One last piece to Merritt's generative resistance worth mentioning had to do with what he believed Parker's motivation was for wanting this type of influence. In Merritt's view, Parker did not really want to learn about Marx but asked for this in order to win Merritt's approval of her. This drove Merritt nuts. That is, if he felt that Parker was truly interested in Marx—*for Marx*—he would probably have welcomed the opportunity to share this part of his world. But since it appeared to him that Parker wanted the engagement as a way to ingratiate herself, Merritt wanted none of it.

> *Merritt*: She's always looking for another task— another way to be good. So then she was going be good intellectually. She said to me, "Oh you should tell me some time about your intellectual history." I said, "Well, it's a long story. I don't know if you really want to know it." [I wanted to say] "It's not necessary for you to know this. You don't have to be a Marxist to be a good person. And you can't be a Marxist just out of fashion. You know, it's out of fashion for Christ sake. And if it doesn't burn in you, it ain't gonna work."

> *Bonnie*: You remember having this chat with her or you're just thinking about it . . .

> *Merritt*: No, I'm thinking about it. But I did have a talk with her once when she said, "Oh I'm a Foucauldian. But I really want to study and become a Marxist." And I said, "People into Foucault are fine. It's okay. You're a good person the way you are. You don't have to . . ."

> *Bonnie*: be you?

> *Merritt*: Yeah! "You don't have to be me."

> *Bonnie*: Somehow there was something not quite authentic in why she wanted to know?

> *Merritt*: Yeah, yeah . . . just curiosity or wanting to sort of place it—like, "Okay, now I understand another *ism*."

In the final analysis, Merritt was very cautious about what kind of person he wanted to share his closely held ideas with because he cared so much about passing on a tradition he loved. Thus, his ambivalence was probably just as much due to the lack of identification he felt with Parker as it was rooted in his passionate and very serious commitment to an intellectual tradition.

* * *

Control and agency

How do mentors take up authority to make an imprint on protégés? How comfortable are they in this role? How do feelings and beliefs about authority in general or about one's own authority in specific, color a mentor's approach to teaching the protégé? Conversations with mentors and protégés show a range of approaches—distinguished with respect to the extent to which a mentor tries (consciously or unconsciously) to create a *clone*, a *path*, a *transitional space*, a *passage*, or operate in a *barren wilderness*. (See Figure 5.2) Though mentors are likely to lean toward one approach as a matter of style, personality, philosophy, or to replicate the way *they* were trained or brought up in a profession, my reason for constructing this typology is not to suggest that mentors fix on a single way of being generative. They do not. Obviously some types of guidance call for more or less supervising authority on the part of the mentor. Teaching the protégé a newly invented surgical technique, for example, would undoubtedly require that the protégé copy an exact protocol taught by a mentor whereas it would probably be more appropriate to take a less directive stance in creative or artistic endeavors. And, of course, things change over time, so while at an early point in a relationship mentors might advise protégés to follow their lead by taking a series of well-tried steps toward professional growth, a mentor might be inclined to hold back at a later point, and encourage a protégé to discover the best avenue to his or her own development. To be more succinct, the goal of the influence usually (ideally) links to the modality. Thus, one should think of the approaches I sketch below as comprising a heuristic framework— varying on a continuum as to how much control the mentor has and how much agency the protégé has in the generativity process. I will also be using the metaphor of reproduction in this discussion to symbolically reference the outcomes that emanate from each approach.

One end of this continuum is—*cloning*—an approach that, in theory, places the mentor in total control, obliterating the self and subjectivity of the protégé. "You can be me," says the mentor whose impulse it is to reproduce him or herself exactly. This collapses two people into one; hence nothing new is birthed. One protégé, high-lighting her mentor's narcissism and difficulty in seeing her as a separate person, put it this way:

> *Pretanya*: Millicent can't really put herself into my head. I mean to her it might be obvious that A, B, or C entails D . . . so she wouldn't even stop to think about whether *I* might respond like that. I mean she has a very strong sense that we see things exactly the same way, that we're sort of

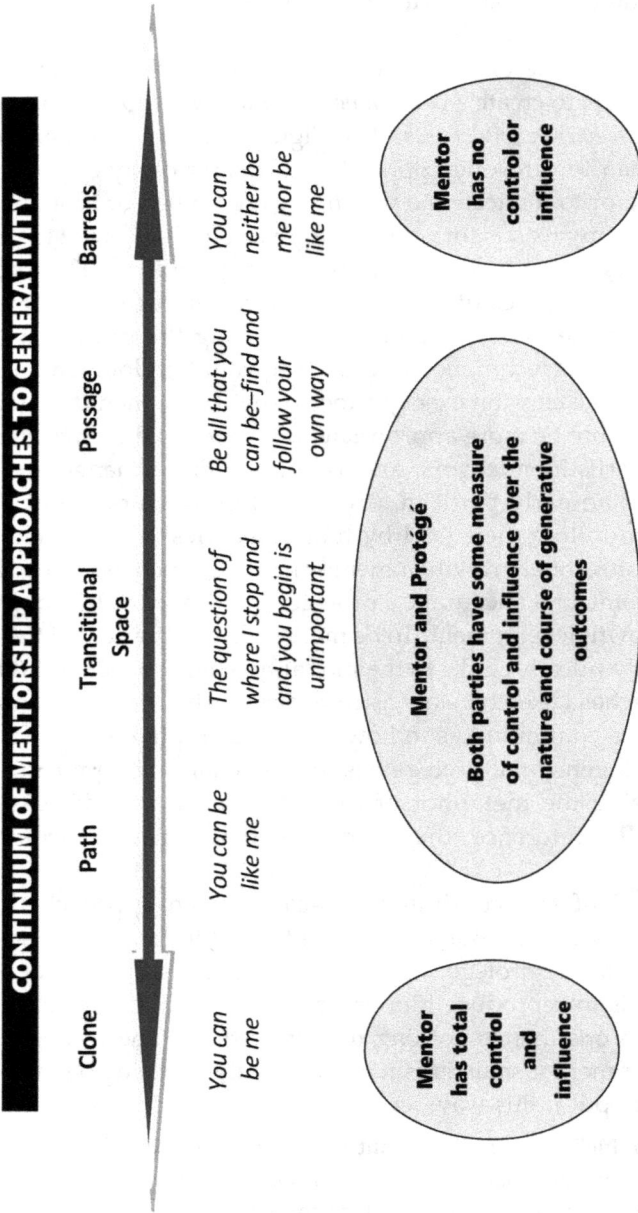

CONTINUUM OF MENTORSHIP APPROACHES TO GENERATIVITY

Clone	Path	Transitional Space	Passage	Barrens
You can be me	*You can be like me*	*The question of where I stop and and you begin is unimportant*	*Be all that you can be—find and follow your own way*	*You can neither be me nor be like me*

Mentor has total control and influence

Mentor and Protégé

Both parties have some measure of control and influence over the nature and course of generative outcomes

Mentor has no control or influence

Figure 5.2

"kindred spirits"—that's how she expressed it to me once . . . I once told her that I thought that when she looked at me, all she saw was a reflection of herself. And that's why there's this discordance between her expectations and what I'm actually able to do . . . I feel like—I'm really exaggerating it—but almost like I'm this mirror. There's nothing behind it, you know, just a pane of glass. When she looks at me—she thinks she's seeing me but what she's seeing is her own strengths and her own abilities and accomplishments.

Millicent actually did seem to have a tough time putting herself into her protégé's shoes. During our conversation, she repeated several times that she believed that Pretanya and she were very much alike—that Pretanya could be just like her at carrying out work at their company and that she could trust her to do so. Millicent became exasperated as it became increasingly clear that her view of Pretanya's abilities was off the mark. Using our interview time largely as an opportunity to talk about and work through her disappointment, Millicent let on that she had always viewed her protégé as her likely successor and she was demoralized as she was beginning to assimilate the idea that Pretanya could not be her replica.

At the other end of the continuum is the approach of *creating a barren wilderness*. Here the protégé's agency is positioned in the forefront and the authority of the mentor is all but erased. The outcome is the flip side of cloning; and as in cloning, no new life is created. But in this case, it is because no seed or gestational support is provided. "You can neither be me nor be like me," says the mentor who cannot or is unwilling to express generative potential. It is as if one holds the belief that the protégé requires no help from the outside to develop. In this sense, there is no mentoring. Perhaps we could view this mode of anti-generativity as a form of contraception—represented by the mentor wants to have the sex (i.e., do the mechanics of mentoring) but refuses to reproduce (i.e., to make something lasting with the protégé). Since my work concerns long-term, thriving mentorships, it is not surprising that I have never met anyone whose generativity or rather, lack of it, falls into this category. A mentor who cannot be generative cannot be expected to last in this role.

It is safe to say that in nearly all cases of mentoring I have come across, the mode of generativity falls somewhere between the two extremes. *"Creating a path"*, *"working in a transitional space"*, and *"creating a passage"* are distinguished from the two extreme ends of the continuum by having an interactional basis. That is, these approaches imagine that two parties are engaged in a give and take process; control is shared and motivation is mutual. The metaphorical outcome is some kind of new life; something grows that did not exist before and its product draws from both mentor and protégé.

In *creating a path*, the mentor maintains some control over the process and outcome but less so than in attempts to clone. The mentor operating in this modality believes that aspects of his or her life and/or work are worth preserving and he or she invites—sometimes insists—that the protégé adopt these things. "You can be like me," says the mentor who creates a path. Looking for someone to "buy into [his] ideas"—one mentor told me that he had set out to find a protégé—a person at the start of his or her career—who would be malleable enough to accept his ideas and "vision."

> *Maury*: I sought out someone who was early enough in their career that I'd almost have a clean slate to work with. I really wouldn't want to work with a seasoned, experienced mentee. I don't want to have to keep tugging at someone to accept the ideas that would help us move forward.

And the strategy seemed to have had some success to hear the protégé tell it:

> *Patina*: Maury steered my career and my personal life. Not in any bossy way. But he helped me to make decisions. I always walked out of his office feeling like I made a decision—he just offered advice. But thinking back—I'm thinking—well, most of those decisions . . . he wanted me to make so he steered me that way! He became a huge force in my life.

Mentors who create a path try to set an example in their conduct, tell stories about their past, use models of teaching to which they were exposed, and have no qualms about being directive in giving advice based on their own experience. These are people who believe strongly that protégés can benefit from going through the same kinds of experiences and training that they went through.

> *Pam*: I don't think emotionally [my mentor] set about entirely consciously to make me A or B. But there are points at which she does. Like she *does* want me to finish my book manuscript—and that's conscious. She tries to kind of manipulate me into thinking that it's really important. And she thinks she's going to have to coax me because she thinks—because

it's for me—that I won't do it . . . Sometimes she'll come out with things (laughs) like that I'm "uptight," that I "don't think about myself enough." She'll just say that directly. And so, when she thinks that she's manipulating me in my best interest, she'll do whatever she can (flashes a smile). And that's conscious.

Here is a case in which the primary generative gift from the mentor was to encourage the protégé to become less self-sacrificing. The protégé acknowledges that she has let a period of time go by without publishing her research, overwhelmed by demands of family, and reluctant to place her own career in the limelight even temporarily, to finish her writing. The idea that women should pay attention to their own needs and interests was a conviction that her mentor had developed as she grew up and uncomfortably watched her mother subordinate her needs to her father. Not to repeat her mother's mistakes, this mentor was almost vigilant not to let her own personhood get lost in marriage and family.

Michele: One thing that I've thought of from pretty early on . . . and my family always teases me about it, is being mean to men. I mean, I've been married three different times. And it was my choice to end those other two marriages . . . Generally, my family has thought of me as somebody who's you know, a "bitch"—to the men she's with. And I agree. That's probably true to some degree. But I very consciously thought that I did not want to have the kind of relationships my mother had with men. I just didn't want to have . . . this, "Whatever makes you happy, honey—if you're interested in it, I'm interested in it; if you say we live here, we live here." You know—the sort of perpetual sense of gratitude to men—absolutely not. (She sighs and laughs) . . .

Bonnie: So you escaped it.

Michele: Oh yeah. I probably went too far in the other direction but that's a different issue . . . That's something I would not do—sacrifice for the guy—You know, my mother put two men through school. As soon as she finished her marriage with my dad, she married a much younger man and put him through dental school after putting my father through law school! . . . So where does she end up? . . . She's a broke high school teacher. Trying to retire and wondering if she's going to have enough money to live.

Given the vagaries of her own life path, one could say that Michele was on a generative mission with Pam—that is, to help her protégé chart a new, less self-depriving juggle of life's priorities. She was "hell-bent" on seeing to it that new generations of women did not defer to the men in their lives—a troubling trend she saw right away as she was getting to know Pam.

In the extreme, mentors who create a path offer protégés a map of how to be, love, and work in the world. Their intellectual, ideological, professional and existential DNA are encoded in generative efforts. The path may have markers, signs, direction, detours, etc.; the important thing is that the path is laid out by and follows a route of the mentor's own life course.

In *creating a passage*, the mentor makes space for the protégé to discover his or her own path and to create something completely new. The emphasis is on the uniqueness of the individual and the provision of support and resources necessary to nurture the flourishing of the individual's potential and choices. "Be all that you can be—find and follow your own way" says the mentor who stays out of the way but tries to ensure that the conditions for natural growth are possible (e.g., providing maximum exposure to a range of ideas, beliefs, alternative skills, and non-judgmental support). This naturalistic approach— where the teacher's role is limited to supervising the environment for learning—mirrors the model of pedagogy set forth in Rousseau's classic book, *Emile* (1964).

Maura illustrates this approach well. Beyond the provision of equipment, studio space, a circuit of colleagues with whom to network, and general cheerleading to Portia, she finds herself "clueless" about how to teach art and expresses great ambivalence about whether that should even be a goal:

> *Maura:* I'm very hesitant to be very forthcoming about "well, you should do this or you should do that," because I have no interest in channeling her or anyone else to write dance pieces like *my* dance pieces. I mean, I choreograph my way and that's my problem. It doesn't really have anything to do with what anybody else wants to do. Obviously if someone came to me and said, "I want to learn how to do this or that movement cause I think it's really cool," of course, I'd be happy to show them how I do it. But that's not what Portia's coming to me to do. And so, it's just a mystery for me. I just don't have a clue what exactly I'm supposed to do. And in some ways—I sort of have this philosophical stance that it's not my job. It's no one's job to tell anybody else how to

choreograph. Whenever that's done, it's either trivial or intrusive—one or the other, you know?

... When she brings me a piece for feedback, I try to tell her what I'm seeing, tell her how I'm understanding her piece, and let her decide on the basis of her knowledge of me and my proclivities, whether she wants to change her piece or not.

... I would like Portia to develop a clear idea of what she herself wants to do. And to whatever degree I can help with that, I'd be delighted to do so. I feel like it's up to her. That is, I don't have any real clear ideas about what I can initiate to help her with that. It's more that she has to initiate what she wants to do in her own life.

At the extreme, offering a passage can lean toward barrenness and is associated with structurelessness. No form exists as a model. Growth is expected to take place in the relative absence of influence as in a kind of void in which the protégé may be offered the basic resources to survive and grow but receives a hands-off, "Do as you please, don't ask me for direction" retreat from mentoring authority and influence.

Somewhere between efforts to creating either a path or a passage lies a way of influencing that might be thought of as an ideal. Here, the line between what results from the mentor's input and what gives rise to the protégé's output is blurred. In this domain of generativity, the mentor and protégé accept ambiguity in the boundaries of influence. It is an intersubjective realm of experience that British psychoanalyst, D. W. Winnicott (1971) called *"transitional space"*—an intermediate zone between "what is objectively perceived and what is subjectively conceived of" (p. 11). In this space, the distinction between what comes from "inside" the person and what comes from "outside" cannot be determined. An example is the appreciation of art or religion, the experiences of which are neither fully created nor discovered. By working in a transitional space, the mentor recognizes his or her authority and the protégé's agency in the same moment. To be generative in this mode means to co-create something new in a way that makes it as impossible to answer as it is irrelevant to ask about who deserves credit for the production.

Paris, a painter mentioned earlier, related many examples of her mentor, Martin's, reactions to her drawings—the very specific ways in which he would offer suggestions about changing the size of the brush, dimensions of the paper, refining lines. He had a light touch in his feedback—merely suggesting things to her that she then would go back and try. Often, they were ideas that she had already been thinking of on her own. Paris would integrate the suggestion—eventually—but in her own way, in her own time. They would be incorporated as her innovations. She said she would find that sometimes it was not clear what was his idea and what was hers. "Often my feeling about the few things he says is that they gel and crystallize things I'm already thinking about and so that afterwards, I can't remember what was his idea and what was mine."

Mentors who conceive of their generative position as an opportunity to create and work in a transitional space with protégés neither wish to clone nor to divest themselves of the authority of knowing or having something to pass on. They neither aggrandize nor negate their own experience and knowledge. In this sense, neither blind obedience, conformity, or indoctrination on the one hand, nor anarchy, structurelessness, or flight from authority on the other hand, are subscribed to, valued, or enacted.

Legitimacy

We have come full circle back to the ambivalent core of mentorship—that is, its authority basis. As I have stressed, it is not uncommon for mentors to have mixed feelings about the legitimacy of their role as authority figures, sometimes leaving them sapped of generative desire. Many talk about feeling burdened by lofty expectations that they put on themselves or are projected by protégés, while others shy away from accepting credit for being an influential person in the lives of protégés. Some equivocate about whether they have anything much to contribute to their protégé's growth; and others feel fraudulent in claiming expertise. Balking at images of themselves as potent authority figures seems to help some mentors keep their generative zeal in check—guarding themselves, perhaps, from the temptation of becoming too grandiose or exploitative.

Occasionally, ideological or moral objections to taking up authority are woven into the emotional ambivalence that mentors experience. Some mentors reflect on their entitlement to authority, or as is being discussed here—the lack of it—calling up repudiated images of authority that have taken hold in American society over the past fifty years. In the previous section, I identified some of the ways that these negative authority images contour the approaches that mentors take in their generativity. Indeed, such images can dissuade mentors from exercising authority altogether. On the one hand are 1960s and post-sixties leftists who rejected authority because of its potential to tilt toward authoritarianism. A few of the older mentors I interviewed who were in college during this turbulent period of American history were adherents of this ideology. From this view, freedom, liberation, growth—call it what you like—comes from dismantling hierarchy and its institutional bases of oppressive thought and practice in capitalism and patriarchy. When pushed to the limit, there is no room in this way of thinking to imagine a conception of authority that is non-authoritarian nor is there room to imagine hierarchy as an expression of difference, not necessarily domination. Not surprisingly, such a belief system poses real challenges for generativity. Marie's articulation of this position was pretty unvarnished; she uses her politically informed objections about "the system" to explain her retreat from authority in relation to her protégé, Patrice:

> *Marie*: As soon as I say that you're the boss, I have to hate ya—cause you're the boss. (She laughs raucously.) That's just the way it is... It's a terrible thing to do, to have your sense of yourself be dependent on authority. Patrice might want this but I won't play along. I think that's a terrible thing to do—and it's odd—especially when radicals do it . . . and they do! . . . Because, on the one hand, we know . . . it's the *system*—hullo? You know, this is it. We know that the scum rises, so what does it really mean when you say, "Am I okay?" You're asking *this* power structure to tell you, "You're okay?"—*this* power structure that is horrid, terrible! . . . In general, I find that a very dangerous stance . . .

On the other side of the same coin are postmodernist skeptics—the most extreme of whom reject the philosophical premise of authority altogether as epistemologically unsound. Truth does not exist, they argue, thus, authority is groundless or tentative and illusory at best. Everyone is his or her own author, we all live inside of language; hence, the idea that anyone could know something of value to pass on to enhance another's life is thought to be capricious and regarded with suspicion. We observed this distrust earlier in Maura's avowed refusal to teach her protégé how to choreograph a dance piece. Similarly, Mischa's attitude about teaching her protégé picks up a postmodern anxiety of influence, again related to creative endeavors:

Mischa: When you have a teaching job, you are an expert. And people come to you. And they say, "So what are the goods?" And you have to then articulate your vision in some reasonably concrete, reasonably consistent, reasonably articulate way which freezes it and prevents you from growing as an artist—or that's my belief. Or that's my fear.

Bonnie: It gets too set in stone?

Mischa: It's too easy if you've got people at your knees trying to learn, trying to master your goods, to think you've got goods. Well, the minute you think you have goods, they aren't goods anymore.

As these brief passages suggest, alongside of the more culturally conservative viewpoints that esteem traditional forms of authority and hierarchy are a historically fluid series of counter-cultural positions. Any of these can play a more or less important role in determining whether there will be generative action or inaction as each provides the mentor with a rationale for either accepting claims to authority or retreating from it.

Adding yet another layer to the obstacles that can impede legitimacy is the changing landscape of work, giving mentors even more pause as they consider the fragile societal context of their authority. As companies reorganize to meet the emerging demands of global and postindustrial economies, well established organizational hierarchies and ways of doing business are being shaken up. This ultimately impacts on generativity. For instance, retooling workplace technology—an activity discussed by several mentors and protégés, and mentioned earlier in the book—often places mentors and protégés on more equal footing regarding technical skills. Inevitably, as the digital world takes over, mentors and protégés both find themselves in the position of learner. Both parties come to depend upon each other— sometimes the mentor is in an even more dependent position, as the protégé, typically more recently trained, is likely to be better versed in the new technology. This reversal encroaches on the image of mentor as the "older and wiser" figure who passes down traditions, routines, and techniques of doing work. While there are relational benefits to leveling authority (e.g., protégés can view mentors as "more human"), old ways of doing business that date the mentors' expertise call into question the relevance of their generative goods and, consequently, the legitimacy of their authority.

Taken together, the cause for a mentor's ambivalent feelings and reservations about embracing the authority role—as it is entailed in generativity—is multi-determined. Beliefs and feelings about authority—the need for it, the legitimacy of it, its value, its perceived hazards, whether one has it, whether one should be subject to it—are emotionally loaded, fueled by transference and linked to fantasies and judgments concerning strength, power, control, expertise, dependency, inexperience, vulnerability, etc. But these things can also be greatly affected by a mentor's personal philosophy and ideological attitudes towards authority, as well as societal events and transformations that impact careers and lives. However resolved or conflicted they are regarding their entitlement to take up authority, mentors need to *feel they have* and *actually do have something* to convey. This is not always a given. And so we turn to explore these issues next.

Legacy

In the final analysis, whether generativity happens at all depends on the extent to which mentors are enfranchised by and invested in creating a legacy. "First you need a sense of belonging to a culture in order to feel responsible to pass it on," wrote Ronald Manheimer (1995, p. 15) in a critical essay about the limits of generativity. At the heart of the matter, thus, are questions about the extent to which mentors have a stake in passing something on to future generations. This partially depends upon whether mentors *feel* a personal connection or claim to ideas, traditions, canons, values, skills, ways of being, etc., or an allegiance to institutions, organisations, or professional fields. Nevertheless, the *psychological investment* in passing something on is only half of the legacy equation. The other half relates to *what is realistically available* in the work culture to be passed on.

Professional satisfaction and success are critical to a mentor's eagerness and sense of responsibility to create a legacy. The extent to which mentors have accomplished their own career goals affects their sense of place in the organization or field in which they work. In turn, this sense of place—of feeling oneself to be a member or leader of an organization or field—fans a mentor's desire and calling to be generative. It stands to reason that mentors will feel more open and hopeful about welcoming protégés into the fold if things have gone well for them—because *they* feel themselves to be a part of that fold. Often people refer to this process as "giving something back" to the organization or profession while inviting protégés to become a part of these communities, to take a seat at the table, so to speak.

Mentors whose careers have gone well also tend to feel more potent and perceive themselves as having more to offer. Of course, this aligns with the fact that they usually *are* better connected and more powerful than mentors whose careers have stagnated or plateaued. Yet a mentor's attitudes about the company or field may be overly idealistic. Grateful for their own ascendance, mentors sometimes suppress the criticisms they used to have about work in earlier days. Success and the resulting sense of affinity to one's field or organization can oblige mentors to toe the party line—that is, to nostalgically defend the traditions, mission, and accomplishments of the company or field somewhat indiscriminately (Gabriel, 1993). Yet that sense of duty, especially when it is bound by orthodox or narrow thinking, can sabotage generativity efforts as we saw with Merritt and Parker, the sociology professors cited earlier.

Mentors who are unsatisfied with their careers or who have been unable to come to terms with thwarted ambitions are not terribly anxious to create legacies, often questioning whether they have the emotional wherewithal to help protégés settle into organizations or fields that have not served them well. Michael, a sports team executive whose career got stunted at middle management, put it this way, "Of course I want Pete to succeed . . . but why would I want him to be thinking long-term in the company—it's a shitty place to work." Verging on sour grapes, this attitude, undoubtedly lines the underbelly of the Salieri phenomenon described earlier. In sum, mentors' perceptions of their generative capacity (e.g., what they *believe* they can offer), their generative desire (e.g., what they *would like* to offer), and the generative reality (e.g., what they *can offer*—practically speaking)—are all informed by career biography—past and present—aspirations and achievements.

*   *   *

Historical, economic, and social structural forces are key to creating and sustaining the conditions in which professional connectedness and legacies either flourish or fade. In this respect, recent work world transformations are enormously important. Due to mergers, downsizings, reorganization schemes, technology conversions, and globalization, individuals are more vulnerable in recent times to career dislocation (Sennett, 2006). Even professional fields—long thought to be sheltered from bottom-line demands—are being reconfigured to gain competitive edge in the marketplace. For generativity, one implication is that learning to manage change and tolerate expendability may now be more valuable legacy skills than elaborating or reproducing tradition.

Indeed, of all of the mentors with whom I have talked over the past twenty years, only about a third had longevity at their jobs. For most, the current job was one of several held over a career. In the public and non-profit sectors, many held positions contingent on soft money—waiting from one fiscal cycle to the next to assure continued employment. In industry, horizontal career moves to avoid stagnation and stay current with professional networks and expertise seemed for many to be the new normal. In the arts, it was not uncommon to hear of mentors employed in freelance day jobs to enable them to pursue relatively low paying creative projects on the side. And as universities roll back opportunities for plum lifetime appointments, mentors, even with tenure, find their hands all but tied in attempts to help protégés attain this kind of job security for themselves.

Given their own transitory ties to organizations and specific jobs, it is easy to understand why mentors might feel neither the desire nor the obligation to groom protégés to carry on institutional traditions. When work life does not function as a cultural envelope—tying individuals to history and to a larger sense of vocational purpose—attachments become fleeting and aspects of generativity can seem irrelevant. Sadly, mounting evidence suggests that many individuals do not feel connected to a professional or institutional home and are provided with little—at least, of cultural value—to pass on to heirs.

Last, but certainly not least, are challenges to legacy-making posed by a mentor's gender and race. Historically blocked from positions of professional power, women and mentors of color who do manage to ascend at work sometimes talk about feeling like "interlopers." Even though they have succeeded at breaking through the proverbial glass ceiling, many lament the fact that they neither feel consistently, nor wholeheartedly, welcomed by colleagues at those echelons. Old boy networks continue to reinforce their marginalization. The fact that a considerable number of female and non-white mentors express reservations about having something to hand down to protégés—

something, that is, that would deepen protégé commitment and sense of belonging to the organizations or professions in which they both work—probably reflects the feeling and unfortunate reality of still being considered an outsider.

* * *

In the classical image, the mentor—traditionally, a man—grooms his protégé—also, traditionally, a man—to be his successor. Influence is geared toward preparing the protégé to fill his shoes, to take over his position when he retires, perhaps even to gradually ease into that position as the mentor scales back his career. The process has a mix of sentimental and political motivations. The mentor wants to induct the protégé into the work world that has become a vocational home to him and to offer his protégé opportunities to step into (his version of) the good life. At the same time, he wants to ensure his legacy is carried forward. After he is gone, the mentor still hopes to wield power through the protégé and through the assertion of his ideals as channeled through the protégé.

Times have changed. Most prominent, of course, is the fact that mentorship is no longer the exclusive province of men. But just as important to the mentorship relation is the fact that we are witnessing profound transformations in the concept of a career. The twentieth century promise of a job for life is no longer the norm nor is the idea that advancement is the outcome of a fairly predictable sequence of vertical moves. Even when they stay in the same company over time, employees are far more likely to make horizontal career moves and undergo job redefinition than they are to advance in a linear progression. Thus, mentors may be able to assist in preparing protégés for future advancement but this is not the same thing as preparing them for *their* jobs in a company or even their positions of stature in a field. *Their* positions are not secure either. If succession is no longer viable, what do mentors groom their protégés for? What can protégés inherit from mentors during this time of great change and uncertainty? These are critical questions as they hint at the penetrating consequences of societal change on relationships like mentorship.

Final thoughts

In this chapter, I have underscored the importance of looking at generativity in mentorship as a dynamic and ambivalent process. Mentors clearly want to influence protégés and pass something on to them in a way that is invested with personal and professional energy. And while internalization is always partial, protégés are usually eager to take in what mentors have to offer. Yet handing something down means letting go of that thing. Even with the best of matches between mentor and protégé, this loss of control itself can create enormous anxiety and consternation.

As examples reveal, however, the process *is* very much dependent on the match between the mentor and protégé. Identification is a linchpin of generativity. Assuming the mentor does have something to hand down and can envision something good becoming of it, he or she can trust the generativity process and engage in it generously. But mentors need to be wary of over-identification—making sure to sort out what protégés might benefit from developmentally or strategically, from their own needs, aspirations, and struggles.

The fact that mentors have mixed feelings and agendas about generativity should not come as a surprise. Mentors experience doubt and sometimes dread at the thought of taking up authority. Some of this is rooted in emotional conflict about one's entitlement to power and the associated responsibilities. I am also convinced, nevertheless, that some of the anxiety is reality-based. That is, the ambivalence of authority is partly a reaction to the fact that professions and organizations are not supplying mentors with the *stuff* to pass on. The vacuum of values and traditions created by post-industrial transience and instability leaves mentors little of cultural import to hand down. Rather than undermining this central function of mentorship, I would like to think that it poses new challenges for redefining generativity in this relationship.

CHAPTER SIX

For the future of mentorship

To end this book, I am going to zoom out to reflect on broader concerns about mentorship as it functions in organizational settings before offering final thoughts about the tenacity and significance of ambivalence in lived mentorships. As I have primarily taken a microscopic look at such relationships and the mixed feelings evoked by them, it is important to step back to assess how such relationships are bred and repurposed in our contemporary world of work, and to take stock of the ways that mentorship could become even more important to culture.

Crafted or produced

At face value, workplace programs that assign individuals to mentoring relationships are to be commended. No one would argue against trying to promote adult support relationships that offer opportunities for professional and personal learning, developmental growth, and empowerment. Likewise, no one or, at least, very few, would argue against trying to promote ideals of social justice and equality in the workplace by leveling the mentorship playing field. Why not offer mentorship to everyone?

There are stark contradictions to be reckoned with as such initiatives proliferate. The first is whether a relationship, like mentorship, which is inherently conservative and elitist can realistically be made available to all. Mentorship's tradition has revolved around the purposeful selection of protégés by mentors, in part, to preserve the homogeneity of various professions and occupations. This gatekeeping system—inviting certain people in while keeping others out—should not be understood to be a mere byproduct of the selection process, but rather fundamental to the mentorship project; at least in its traditional, classic form. In this sense, mentorship can rightly be blamed for playing a role in perpetuating discriminatory practices in professional life (see Epstein et al., 1995). All the same, mentorship has not been conceived of, nor has it ever pretended to be, democratic—either in the context of the micro-level, interpersonal, authority-based relation between mentor and protégé, or in the wider context as an alliance between two people amid a host of competitive actors in organizations and professions. Hence, all employees or professionals could not possibly benefit from getting a "leg up." Even if we could imagine this—that everyone would get a leg up—would not that imply that no one actually does?

Considering the argument that I have been making throughout this book about the centrality of an emotional connection to mentorship, it is even more difficult to imagine how democratizing this relation could work. Trying to engineer relationships based on the universalistic premise that all are entitled to and should be offered a chance to work with a mentor probably would, as I indicated in the chapter on loyalty, bump up against the particularistic dynamics of attachment that give mentorship its lifeblood. How, for example, could bonding agents like idealization, loyalty, or generativity do their job in a mentorship that is arranged by a workplace program founded on the principle of evenhanded treatment to all employees? Such a proposition would be like trying to mandate that one should care for all children, not just one's own—overlooking the bias intrinsic to emotional attachment. Put another way, if we are not built to admire or idealize everyone (or just anyone), and if we do not feel the urge to be loyal or generative to everyone (or just anyone), then how can produced mentorships be "fair?" Emotions of attachment like these develop in relationships with particular people. Even if one is committed to the goal of impartiality, it is a stretch to think that emotional bonding in mentorship could be decreed, let alone applied to all.

Beyond concerns about equity are more practical matters of fit: how can planners of mentoring programs be expected to design viable pairing schemes when, as has been well documented, there is so much beneath the surface, indeed, a good deal of it unconscious—emotionally, intellectually, ideologically, strategically, and politically—that determines the potential for a good match? Though we do understand some of the elements of good chemistry in mentorship, relationships are not science experiments. Perhaps going the route of advertising for a mentor or protégé in personal ads or on a web-based social media site might not be such a quirky idea after all.

I am not suggesting that human resources managers throw up their hands because they might not be able to create ideal mentorship pairings or programs. The options for democratizing mentorship, however, must entail reining in expectations and adjusting ideas about how mentorship can be beneficial once institutionalized. Many people do begin mentorship alliances organically—starting as bosses or supervisors and subordinates, or like myself, being assigned to work as a research assistant with my first professor mentors. Mentorships can take off from such institutional pairings. Yet, if the goal is to correct workplace inequalities by lining up mentorship matches, structuring the mentoring activity, and monitoring progress, then such relations will face trouble moving past bureaucratic trappings. I have heard of far too many programs like this. The alliances succeed on paper—in satisfying company reports of activity aimed at promoting diversity, but this usually has little to do with mentorship. Even while recent studies show that affirmative action and diversity initiatives like mentoring reduce social isolation of women and minorities (Kalev et al., 2006), and that "high quality" mentorships—including those assembled through workplace programs—cushion protégés from the stresses of discriminatory workplaces (Ragins et al., 2016), there is little evidence that such programs actually do much to remediate structural inequalities.

Essentially, what I am raising here as I have in previous chapters, is the core difference between mentorship and other types of less intensive support relationships such as coaching, sponsoring, and advising. Workplace programs can definitely be helpful in structuring these types of latter relationships; they are more concrete in the types of assistance offered, more empirically researchable and assessable—and in an era of hyper-accountability, organizations certainly like that feature, and little commitment is expected of the parties beyond trying to meet contractual goals. Putting aside the possibility that such relationships might flourish on their own after having been initially formed through a mentoring program template—it is important that companies acknowledge the limits as to what formally arranged relationships can do for career advancement, adult development, professional positioning, and for the sense of cultural connectedness that I have called attention to a number of times in the book.

*   *   *

Even when good matches are made, there are risks in putting all of one's eggs in one mentor basket—that is, in pursuing a traditional exclusive one-to-one mentorship. Perhaps I have been frivolous to go on so much about the challenges of creating meaningful mentorship relationships through workplace programs, considering the times in which we live and work. Fragmentation and instability characterize current trends in work. Jobs are not secure, career paths are not predictable. Given the uncertainty and transience, why advocate for the development of exclusive long term mentorships? Are they not likely to break off, as I have already described in a few cases—my own included? And do such partings hurt careers?

To hear Patrick tell it, the answer is yes. A mid-level manager in computer services at a large law firm, Patrick talked to me about "getting burned" by allowing himself to tie his kite to a mentor who suddenly quit his job. In the aftermath, Patrick was not only left without a dependable supporter and confidante, but his own future at the firm was upended. He could no longer count on advancing to a position that his mentor had lead him to believe was his for the taking. Lulled into a state of complacency, Patrick told me he had ignored opportunities to work with other potential allies in his department and never gave a thought to the possibility that his career chances might be jeopardized if his mentor left. He was stunned when it happened. At the time of our conversation, Patrick was still steaming about having "set himself up" this way, as though the mentorship alliance was a "mirage" that left him feeling duped and abandoned.

There are obvious perils to settling in with one mentoring partner at work. That said, it is not empirically clear that the alternative—that is, having loads of senior colleagues and peers in one's network or a handful of less intensive coaches or sponsors—can or should supplant the more classic version of mentorship. Though it sounds logical that the more contacts one has, the greater the access to a diversity of opportunities, "weak ties"—to use a term coined by Granovetter (1973)—cannot be relied upon to provide the quality, vigor, and proactive kind of assistance that significant mentorships offer. Still, one should not be too cavalier about relying upon one person to shepherd him or her through a career. If one can negotiate the complex feelings of competition, jealousy, and triangulation dilemmas that may ensue from playing the field, having a combination of a strong classic mentorship plus a wide-ranging network of professional contacts is probably a prudent strategy to cover one's bases.

Anchoring

Many have observed that modernity brought with it a loss of community and links between individuals. As care was replaced by consumerism, we experienced what Lasch (1979) and others noted to be a shift from concern for others to concern for the self and things, and a move away from attention to means to an obsession with ends. More recently, postmodern thinkers have taken this bleak view of individualism and commodification a disturbing step further—suggesting that concern itself has become facile. Switching identities and deconstructing and reconstructing narratives as ways of talking about ourselves superficially brought us into an era where the very idea of shared meaning is in question.

The latter point touches on Richard Sennett's central concern in *The Corrosion of Character* (1998). He blames flexible capitalism, specifically, for a growing sense of social alienation. In an evolving postindustrial system, he argues, individuals are deprived from having a semblance of stability, coherence, and meaningfulness in their work lives. People become piece workers in an economy in which organizations cannot promise long term loyalty or commitment to employees. Boundaryless careers—where individuals are no longer connected long term to organizations, shuttling from one job to the next—erode the social anchoring function of work and organizations. The net result is that individuals are adrift—delinked from their location in culture and history. There is loss of a sense of larger purpose to which people can subscribe and with that, Sennett laments, a loss of historical narrative. Such atomism makes it difficult to frame experience and understand one's life story as connected to history—not isolated from the macro world of culture, the economy, politics, and other social structures.

I want to suggest that as a flourishing social relation, mentorship has challenged these trends even while it has also had to adapt to them. Concern for others and meaning are alive and well in this relationship. And it is not just within the family or private sphere where scholars of modernism predicted that we would retreat. Mentorship bridges the public and private domains—at its best, offering an emotionally enriched learning experience, political access, material resources, developmental guidance, and connection to a legacy from which to continue to build and live out a fulfilling work and personal life.

Organizations and professions also gain a tremendous amount from these alliances as senior colleagues help junior colleagues adapt, progress, and contribute to their companies and fields, however transitory these affiliations turn out to be. Moreover, because they can outlive institutional attachments, mentorships serve the world of work in general as they help ease the stresses of job uncertainty and stabilize individuals in professional ties—badly needed to keep them connected to communal life and to matters apart from the everyday routines of individual existence.

The emotionally complicated processes that drive mentorship must be seen in the context of these large scale changes in the work world. To know that people feel insecure in their jobs and professional futures may help explain why the attachments in mentorship become so fierce and important. Given its constitutional ambiguity and ambivalence, it does seem ironic that people may in fact be clinging to mentorship for mooring during precarious times. It may also be the case that since jobs and careers are transitory, individuals in mentorship draw in closer—feeling the threat of separation as a reminder of the need to make the most of the relationship while it lasts.

Limits and possibilities

I came to this work with a belief that mentorship can be a uniquely satisfying and productive relationship, reaching across what is often felt to be a chasm between the professional and the personal. After decades of research, I retain this belief. There is more than ample evidence that much good can come from these relationships. Mentors and protégés cast these alliances as pivotal, often impacting their lives in life-changing ways. Still, because deep relationships are in some sense, paradoxically ephemeral, occurring fluidly over time without deliberate breaks to notice their effects or even their ordinary flow, many are hard pressed to articulate how or when intense feelings took off, expectations and obligations set in, and influence took hold. And because of the heft of the title and the ambiguity of the relation's form, mentorships sometimes live under the radar as role partners equivocate about stating the importance of their connection. It is the naming and the cognitive framing—call it the meta-life about the mentorship—that hangs some people up, however, not the actual content of the relationship. Indeed, in free-wheeling conversation, mentors and protégés easily acknowledge the gifts of knowledge, insight, skill, technique, social and political capital, emotional support, life guidance, connection to a larger sense of purpose, and of course, friendship, as well as love, trust, and respect that are given and received in a reciprocal fashion. The pleasures and benefits are bi-directional, in spite of *and* because of the fundamental power difference between mentor and protégé.

Some observe that mentorship offers second chances for parties to bond in ways that they missed out on earlier in life. This certainly resonates with the potency of feeling expressed by individuals involved in such relationships. While it is true that clinical training sensitized my ability to listen for latent meaning, one need not be a psychoanalyst to detect an indelible layering of transference in mentorship. Old longings and anxieties are roused and revisited, sometimes like old pests and other times like old friends, but often as opportunities to grow up again. All of that being said, the thrust of the book—its *raison d'être*—has been to take a deep dive into the myriad ways that bonds of mentorship pivot to be the very thing that produce its binds. And as it seems, one cannot not have it both ways.

Throughout the course of this exploration, I have tried to show how emotionally dear and fraught mentorship is. As a relationship forged at the intersection of authority and love, my aim has been to closely inspect and shed light on the ways in which ambivalence is hardwired into the relationship. It is *not* something that occurs when things go wrong. Indeed, it can be a sign that things are going right.

Approaching mentorship with an eye on its complexity resets the misleading trend in contemporary literature of splitting the positive and negative "sides" of the relation, myopically focusing on one side or the other. Missing the boat in this way, Fineman (2000) rightly notes, is part of a broader problem in organizational research,

> Arguably the notion that our work lives are characterized by divisions of positive and negative feelings is a convenient social narrative. It permits the presentation of one's messy or inchoate feelings in any easy linguistic "package," a format with which some social scientists are content to collude. (p. 13)

Exploring the emotional landscape of mentorship, thus, involves not only looking at the good and the bad, but more importantly, mapping out the interrelatedness of these so-called "sides." Mentor–protégé stories recounted in this book affirm the value of taking this turn in research, as they offer compelling testimony about the dialectical nature of intimacy in these relationships. They point to the ways that idealization, admiration, and reverence sow the seeds of dependence, envy, disillusionment, and disappointment. They illustrate how loyalty and devotion sow the seeds of conformity, infidelity, and betrayal—binding mentors and protégés in ways that curb autonomy, voice, and freedom. And they reveal how generativity, the desire and efforts to influence, and to engage in creative collaboration sow the seeds of competition, loss of control, and fears of obsolescence. It should be underscored that such findings are not from extraordinary mentorship accounts. Though it is true that many examples presented in the book have a dramatic quality—purposefully so, ambivalent dynamics run throughout all the stories, however muted the descriptions of their enactments and expression.

For the purpose of summarizing: we now have a more fleshed out understanding of how idealization inspires and distorts. On the one hand, mentors are viewed as beacons of—*hope*—promoting striving, risk-taking, hard work, faith in the future, and openness to learning. We read in Chapter Three about protégés who put their mentors on pedestals—going to great lengths to try to please and emulate them, yet later resented that their own professional identities had been squelched, in some cases worrying that colleagues viewed them as mere appendages of the mentor. Puffed up images of mentors lead to unrealistic expectations imposed not only on the mentor, but then carrying over to the protégé. This was especially true of protégés who saw their mentors as magicians—amazed by their seemingly super-human gifts—sparking enthusiasm and drive to become as wise and powerful as their mentors appeared to be. Filled with self-doubt and feeling inferior by comparison, some protégés took this fantasy as a sign that they should give up. Others were moved, albeit defensively, to try to catch up to their seemingly magical mentor by imitating them in the most superficial ways, hoping to bypass the hard work of personal and career development. In some instances, these turns of idealization put mentors off, or raised anxieties or judgments about dependency, other times it indulged the mentors' sense of grandiosity or gave them license to exploit.

We also have a better picture of how loyalty bonds and binds. This is based on a good deal of evidence that as the glue of mentorship, loyalty connects and confines. In Chapter Four, we see mentors and protégés going to great lengths to stand by each other and demonstrate their allegiance to seeing the relationship last and thrive. This included stories from protégés who devoted themselves and were wholeheart-edly loyal to their mentors, taking enormous pleasure interacting from within a bubble of care and protection amid the aggressive maneuver-ings of professional and organizational life, later to discover that by doing so, they had sheltered themselves from noticing their mentor's flaws, or cut themselves off from opportunities to branch out to learn or access resources from other colleagues or would-be advisors. Displaying their loyalty, we have heard from protégés who labored for mentors—sometimes materially in carrying out unpleasant or tedious work, but most often emotionally, in the enactment of caretaking and buffering roles to show deference, appreciation, and payback for the mentors' ardent efforts to stick by them. Not infrequently did such labor exact a toll from protégés whose cover for mentors some-times caused them to lose face with colleagues or subordinates, or to other diminishing or self-sabotaging behaviors. We have seen that these kinds of ritualized acts of loyalty run the risk of suppressing dissent, constricting the free flow of ideas and relationships, and provoking jealousy and suspicion among colleagues. Like their coun-terparts, mentors also felt the binds as they tried to stay loyal to their trusted protégés, especially racking when the latter failed to live up to initial hopes or expectations that mentors had, but almost always charged when protégés posed political or reputational risks for the mentor.

And finally, we gained insight about how generativity entails giving and loss. Depicted in Chapter Five, this dynamic had its most poignant expression in conversations with mentors who confided that although they had felt genuine desire to teach, make an imprint, and create a legacy, they also felt wary about doing so—aware that they were having trouble letting go of and passing on to protégés—ideas, insights, tips, pearls of wisdom, access to important people, networks, symbolic or material resources—things that were most meaningful to them and things they strived hard to attain for themselves. They related that they were careful about what, when, and to whom they would convey the stuff of their influence, anxious about the potential of having that stuff be misrepresented by a protégé, guilty about urges to compete with protégés who are rising, insecure about their own adequacy and having something of value to offer, and afraid of being rendered irrelevant.

*   *   *

Must ambivalence be resolved? The short answer is yes, no, and maybe. Extreme ambivalence can lead to incapacitating states of excessive rumination, mental or emotional paralysis (Ashforth et al., 2014), and exhausting vacillation—leading one to act in erratic ways tied to the fluctuations of feeling. This can make it nearly impossible for a person to make critical decisions, act on their own behalf, or stabilize relationships. Resolution is surely required for relief as well as for the ability to move out of a stuck or self-defeating position. In long term emotionally bonded mentorships—the kind that I study—I have not seen this kind of suffering. I suspect that mentors or protégés who might be prone to experiencing ambivalence at such acute levels would not be able to sustain the connection—thus, they would not have made it into my study. We do hear the occasional story about relationships where mentors and protégés act out in histrionic swings of highs and lows—seesawing from slavish devotion to vengeful betrayal, for example. These are not the types of mentorship that I studied or that I set out to study.

On this point, I do acknowledge that my research can be taken to task for its obvious gaps. My decision to study continuous, long-term mentorships built in a self-selection bias towards sturdy, matured relationships. This all but precluded an exploration of the conditions under which ambivalent strains might lead to a breakup or to a failure to take off in the first place. Left unexamined are the kinds of emotional pressures that cannot be sustained. I deliberately chose to study long-lasting mentorships to find out what holds them together. What leads to their demise clearly deserves equal attention. Studies of fractured and terminated relationships should be pursued to trace the role of emotional conflict in endings.

All of that being said, studying mentors and protégés in relatively healthy relationships does make one question claims about the alleged dysfunctionality of ambivalence. Emerging research in the psychology of workplace relationships, in fact, indicates that ambivalence can lead to positive outcomes. For example, some studies show that ambivalence makes people more likely to take the perspective of others, and leads people to make better decisions (Rothman & Melwani, 2016). Seeing things from other people's point of view, that is, allows one to see more sides of an issue, allowing one to fully think through the issue before coming to a decision. Ambivalence, that is, provides opportunities to wrestle with difference.

In addition to enhanced empathy and decision-making, being able to tolerate opposing feelings, pushes and pulls, tensions, and conflict is interpersonally adaptive. It can even strengthen rather than harm our most important relationships. In the face of uncertainty, the ability to handle anxious feelings, to be able to live with unresolved questions, and still press on and move forward—is a skill set picked up on by several authors who posit that ambivalence underlies some of our most enduring commitments (e.g., Brickman et al., 1987). Indeed, they argue that doubt—the grist of ambivalence—is what prompts people to make commitments. That is to say, if there is no doubt about one's connection to another person or cause, the connection is simply taken for granted. Consequently, there is no need to think about, devote oneself to, or cognitively or emotionally invest oneself in the establishment or maintenance of a commitment.

As we mull over this paradox—that doubt is what keeps us steady in relationships—it makes sense to ask how mentors and protégés manage their doubts to stay the course. To that end, rather than looking to see how pairs resolve mentorship tensions and difficulties, I have tried to get at how they negotiate them. Even if it was a goal, there is something about the notion of "resolving" ambivalence—as if this could be done once and for all, and completely at that—that does not synch up with the ways in which mentors and protégés talk about handling the tensions in their relationships. So when I say *negotiate*, I mean this in the same way that a gymnast is said to negotiate steps on a balance beam; she maneuvers in a space in which gravity is always pulling in one direction or another yet she resists the oscillations so she can stay on the beam. Likewise for mentorship, the ambiguous structure and ambivalent dynamics exert contradictory tugs and interject uncertainty into the alliance, creating fine lines that mentors and protégés need to traverse if they are to hang in there and take what is good from the relationship—even if it is not everything.

Even if it is not everything. Beyond the tangible career advances and professional growth that can come from mentorship, the process of working through difficult feelings, making peace with the imperfections of the other person, coming to terms with the limits of one's control, and grasping what functions mentorship can and cannot serve is its own benefit. Protégés come to realize that mentors cannot and will not deliver a work life of ease—forever standing by and protecting them, generously passing along gems of their personal wisdom and professional capital. And as the relation unfolds, mentors see that protégés cannot and will not always admire or accept their influence and will move on (especially if they have done a good job) and leave them behind. The growth process as the relationship evolves and each party's maturation as a result of staying the course to work things out is itself an important mentorship function with its own developmental value. This also includes being able to appraise the relationship and walk away when it is clear that one can or must separate. In this sense, mentorship is no different from any other significant life relationship. When things go well, one could say that mentorship's contribution to human relations is that each party comes to appreciate that we cannot be all things to all people.

> The disappointed self is able to recognize what cannot be changed and learn from it; in fact such learning is part of the disappointment, and it involves the recognition of one's own shadow, the integration of the "bad" parents, and through this the recognition of one's own limitations. (Craib, 1994, p. 176)

In his gutsy and highly original book, *The Importance of Disappointment* (1994), Ian Craib heralds this theme as a corrective to late modern society's proclivity toward cheerful optimism, in the tendency to hold out hope for perfectly attuned and responsive partnerships, and in bromides about quick-fix solutions to problems that normally involve struggle and are unpredictable in their course. The thought that everything will be better and can be made to be better is an illusion, Craib argues, as it denies our very real human vulnerabilities and limitations. Accepting the limits of one's role partner is part of the process of coming to terms with and learning from disappointment. *This* is perhaps the most freeing lesson that mentorship has to offer.

* * *

What does it say to us then, that despite the ambivalence and uncertainty built into and surrounding the mentoring relation in the work world at large, people continue to seek out and hold on to these relationships, often over long periods of time? For a long time, this baffled me—yet, after having drawn the dots between doubt and commitment, it is starting to make sense.

One might predict that the ambiguity in mentorship would create too much confusion between parties, or give rise to too much emotional tension or cognitive dissonance, or that somehow people would regard these relationships as fleeting and move in and out of them casually. Or that the ambiguity would lead to a low stakes orientation to the relationship. That is to say, because the norms, roles, and boundaries of mentorship are so nebulous, individuals might not feel social pressure to stay in them, work on them, try to nurture and develop them, or hope to benefit by them in anything more than superficial ways.

Early in the book I allude to the possibility that because there is freedom to define the terms of mentorship—owing to the fact that commitments and obligations are not clearly articulated—individuals may, paradoxically, find themselves compelled to pursue and maintain mentorship attachments. I now find this to be an even more compelling hypothesis. In my view, the fact that mentorship is not conventionalized—that parties are relatively unencumbered by social rules or expectations to make of it what they want—gives it a vitality lacking in formal or more precisely scripted social relationships. The freedom to walk away from a mentorship, to dissolve the alliance may be an ingredient that keeps parties interested, creative, and curious about what next they can accomplish together.

REFERENCES

Ashforth, B. E., Rogers, K. M., Pratt, M. G., & Pradies, C. (2014). Ambivalence in organizations: a multilevel approach. *Organization Science, 25*: 1453–1478.

Ayres, A. (1884). *The Mentor: A Little Book for the Guidance of Such Men and Boys as Would Appear to Advantage in the Society of Persons of the Better Sort*. New York: Funk & Wagnalis.

Baum, H. S. (1992). Mentoring: narcissistic fantasies and oedipal realities. *Human Relations, 45*: 223–245.

Benjamin, J. (1995). *Like Subjects, Love Objects*. New Haven, CT: Yale University Press.

Bleuler, E. (1910). Vortag uber ambivalenz. *Zentralblatt fur Psychoanalyse, 1*.

Bloom, H. (1973). *The Anxiety of Influence*. New York: Oxford University Press.

Brickman, P., Janof-Bulman, R., & Rabinowitz, V. C. (1987). Meaning and value. In: C. B. Wortman & R. Sorrentino (Eds.), *Commitment, Conflict, and Caring* (pp. 59–105). Englewood Cliffs, NJ: Prentice-Hall.

Callahan, J. L., & McCollum, E. E. (2002). Conceptualizations of emotion research in organizational contexts. *Advances in Developing Human Resources, 1*: 4–21.

Carew, J. (1999). *The Mentor*. New York: Penguin Putnam.

Carruthers, J. (1993). The principles and practice of mentoring. In: B. J. Caldwell & E. Carter (Eds.), *The Return of the Mentor: Strategies for Workplace Learning* (pp. 9–24). London: Falmer Press.

Chasseguet-Smirgel, J. (1985). *The Ego Ideal: A Psychoanalytic Essay on the Malady of the Ideal*, P. Burrows (Trans.). New York: W. W. Norton.

Coles, R. (1993). *The Call of Service: A Witness to Idealism*. New York: Houghton Mifflin.

Collins, E., & Scott, P. (1978). Everyone who makes it has a mentor. *Harvard Business Review, 54*: 89–101.

Craib, I. (1994). *The Importance of Disappointment*. London: Routledge.

Duck, S. (1995). Talking relationships into being. *Journal of Social and Personal Relationships, 12*: 535–540.

Eisenstadt, S. N., & Roniger, L. (1984). *Patrons, Clients and Friends*. Cambridge: Cambridge University Press.

Epstein, C. F., Sauté, R., Oglensky, B., & Gever, M. (1995). Glass ceilings and open doors: women's advancement in the legal profession. *Fordham Law Review, 64*(2): 200–360.

Ettinger, E. (1995). *Hannah Arendt and Martin Heidegger*. New Haven, CT: Yale University Press.

Fineman, S. (2000). Emotional arenas revisited. In: S. Fineman (Ed.), *Emotion in Organizations* (2nd edn) (pp. 1–24). London: Sage.

Flam, H. (1993). Fear, loyalty, and greedy organizations. In: S. Fineman (Ed.), *Emotion in Organizations* (1st edn) (pp. 58–75). London: Sage.

Fletcher, G. P. (1993). *Loyalty: An Essay on the Morality of Relationships*. New York: Oxford University Press.

Freud, S. (1912b). The dynamics of transference. *S. E., 12*: 97–108. London: Hogarth.

Freud, S. (1914c). On narcissism: an introduction. *S. E., 14*: 67–102. London: Hogarth.

Freud, S. (1923d). A seventeenth-century demonological neurosis. *S. E., 19*: 67–106. London: Hogarth.

Gabriel, Y. (1993). Organisational nostalgia—reflections on "The golden age". In: S. Fineman (Ed.), *Emotion in Organizations* (1st edn) (pp. 118–141). London: Sage.

George, D. H. (1994). A vision of my obscured soul. *The Ohio Review, 51*: 41–52.

Granovetter, M. (1973). The strength of weak ties. *American Journal of Sociology, 78*: 1360–1380.

Grimes, T. (2010). *Mentor: A Memoir*. Portland, OR: Tin House.

Hirschman, A. O. (1970). *Exit, Voice and Loyalty*. Cambridge, MA: Harvard University Press.

Hochschild, A. R. (1983). *The Managed Heart: Commercialization of Human Feeling*. Berkeley, CA: University of California Press.

Homer (1996). *The Odyssey*, R. Fagles (Trans.) and B. Knox (Introduction and notes). New York: Penguin.

Huang, C. A., & Lynch, J. (1995). *Mentoring: The Tao of Giving and Receiving Wisdom*. New York: Harper Collins.

Josselson, R. (1996). *The Space Between Us: Exploring the Dimensions of Human Relationships*. Thousand Oaks, CA: Sage.

Kalev, A., Kelly, E., & Dobbin, F. (2006). Best practices or best guesses? Assessing the efficacy of corporate affirmative action and diversity policies. *American Sociological Review*, 71: 589–617.

Kanter, R. M. (1977). *Men and Women of the Corporation*. New York: Basic Books.

Kets de Vries, M. F. R. (1980). *Organisational Paradoxes: Clinical Approaches to Management*. London: Tavistock.

Klein, M. (1986[1946]). Notes on some schizoid mechanisms. In: J. Mitchell (Ed.), *The Selected Melanie Klein* (pp. 176–200). New York: Free Press.

Kotre, J. (1996). *Outliving the Self: How We Live on in Future Generations*. New York: W. W. Norton.

Kram, K. (1988). *Mentoring at Work: Development Relationships in Organizational Life*. Lanham, MD: University of America Press.

Lady, By a. (1851). *The Young Lady's Mentor: A Guide to the Formation of Character. In a Series of Letters to Her Unknown Friends*. Philadelphia, PA: H. C. Peck and Theo Bliss.

Lasch, C. (1979). *The Culture of Narcissism: American Life in an Age of Diminishing Expectations*. New York: W. W. Norton.

Lazar, D. (1994). On mentorship. *The Ohio Review*, 51: 25–33.

Lerner, A. J., & Loewe, F. (1956). *My Fair Lady: A Musical Play in Two Acts*. New York: Signet.

Levinson, D. J., with Darrow, C. N., Klein, E. B., Levinson, M. H., & McKee, B. (1978). *The Seasons of a Man's Life*. New York: Ballantine.

Lopate, P. (1994). Terror of mentors. *The Ohio Review*, 51: 102–111.

Lorber, J. (1979). Trust, loyalty, and the place of women in the informal organization of work. In: J. Freeman (Ed.), *Women: A Feminist Perspective* (pp. 347–355). Palo Alto, CA: Mayfield.

Lorber, J. (1984). *Women Physicians: Careers, Status, and Power*. New York: Tavistock.

Manheimer, R. J. (1995). Redeeming the aging self: John Kotre, George Drury, and cultural generativity. *Journal of Aging Studies*, 9: 13–20.

Oglensky, B. D. (2008). The ambivalent dynamics of loyalty in mentorship. *Human Relations, 61*: 419–448.

Oglensky, B. D. (2010). The "M" word: fears and fantasies. *Clio's Psyche, 16*: 391–395.

"Publisher wanted for mentor/friendship with creative woman—w4m (Philadelphia suburbs)" *Craigslist.* www.philadelphia.craigslist.org/stp/6149158311.html (accessed 31 May 2017).

Ragins, B. R., Ehrhardt, K., Lyness, K. S., Murphy, D. D., & Capman, J. F. (2016). Anchoring relationships at work: high-quality mentors and other supportive work relationships as buffers to ambient racial discrimination. *Personnel Psychology, 70*: 1211–1256.

Reza, Y. (1996). *Art,* C. Hampton (Trans.). London: Faber & Faber.

Rothman, N. B., & Melwani, S. (2016). Feeling mixed: ambivalent, and in flux: the social functions of emotional complexity for leaders. *Academic of Management Review, 42*: 259–282.

Rousseau, J. J. (1964). *Emile.* Woodbury, NY: Barron's Educational Series.

Royce, J. (1908). *The Philosophy of Loyalty.* New York: MacMillan.

Salzberger-Wittenberg, I., Williams, G., & Osborne, E. (1999). *The Emotional Experience of Learning and Teaching.* London: Karnac.

Scandura, T. A. (1998). Dysfunctional mentoring relationships and outcomes. *Journal of Management, 24*: 449–467.

"seeking mentor—m4m (Midtown West)" *Craigslist.* www.newyork.craigslist.org/mnh/stp/6185 682982.html (accessed 27 June 2017).

Sennett, R. (1980). *Authority.* New York: Random House.

Sennett, R. (1998). *The Corrosion of Character: The Personal Consequences of Work in the New Capitalism.* New York: Norton.

Sennett, R. (2006). *The Culture of the New Capitalism.* New Haven, CT: Yale University Press.

Shaw, G. B. (1916). *Pygmalion.* New York: Brentano.

Silver, C. B., & Spilerman, S. (1990). Psychoanalytic perspectives on occupational choice and attainment. *Research in Social Stratification and Mobility, 9*: 181–214.

Simmel, G. (1950). Secrecy. In: *The Sociology of Georg Simmel,* K. H. Wolff (Ed., Trans., and Introduction by) (pp. 330–344). New York: The Free Press.

Simmons, T. (1994). *Erotic Reckoning: Mastery and Apprenticeship in the Work of Poets and Their Lovers.* Urbana, IL: University of Illinois Press.

Smelser, N. (1998). The rational and the ambivalent in the social sciences: 1997 Presidential address for the American Sociological Association. *American Sociological Review, 63*: 1–16.

Tyler, K., & Drake, J. (2014). *Mentor Spirit Cards*: *Implementing Change Through Innovation Actions*. Lithia Springs, GA: World Tree Press. Available at: www.bookdepository.com/Mentor-Spirit-Cards-Kathy-Tyler/9780975476208

Webster Ninth New Collegiate Dictionary (1986). Springfield, MA: Merriam-Webster.

Winnicott, D. W. (1971). *Playing and Reality*. London: Tavistock.

INDEX

For Product Safety Concerns and Information please contact our EU
representative GPSR@taylorandfrancis.com
Taylor & Francis Verlag GmbH, Kaufingerstraße 24, 80331 München, Germany